Overshadowed: Leonardo da Vinci and Bernardino Luini

David Alan Brown

Overshadowed

Leonardo da Vinci and Bernardino Luini

SKIRA

Cover
Bernardino Luini, *Pietà*, detail
Private collection

Design
Luigi Fiore

Editorial coordination
Emma Cavazzini

Copy editor
Andrew Ellis

Layout
Sara Marcon

Iconographic research
Paola Lamanna

First published in Italy in 2022 by
Skira editore S.p.A.
Palazzo Casati Stampa
via Torino 61
20123 Milano
Italy
www.skira.net

Printed and bound in Italy.
First edition

ISBN: 978-88-572-4805-9

Distributed in USA, Canada, Central & South America by
ARTBOOK | D.A.P.
75 Broad Street, Suite 630,
New York, NY 10004, USA.
Distributed elsewhere in the world by Thames and Hudson Ltd.
181A High Holborn, London
WC1V 7QX, United Kingdom.

Contents

Written during the coronavirus pandemic, this book examines a selection of paintings by Bernardino Luini that were influenced by Leonardo da Vinci. Comparative analysis shows that Luini, from adopting Leonardo's compositions and motifs, went on to incorporate elements of his style and expression in a group of works dating to the 1520s. These are the focus of the book. In imitating Leonardo, Luini traded complexity for clarity, simplifying his manner and making it accessible to a broad audience undifferentiated by age, gender, or class. The artist's method of popularizing Leonardo, however, led to criticism of his works as merely derivative, but that fails to consider their function as devotional images. Beyond church teachings and practices, little is known about how ordinary viewers looked at religious art in this period.[1] Their responses are not recorded. But Luini's paintings themselves provide clues, like the foregrounding of the figures and their interaction with each other and the beholder, to indicate how they served a devotional purpose. The artist may not have been an intellectual like Leonardo, but the thinking inherent in his works is absolutely coherent and consistent. Their clear organization and unequivocal meaning effectively communicate the religious message he sought to convey.

In addition to the individuals thanked in the notes, the author would like to express his gratitude for help received from the following colleagues at the National Gallery of Art, Washington, DC, where he served as Curator of Italian and Spanish Paintings: Gwendolyn Androsko, Salima Appiah Duffell, Kathy Bordwell, Charlotte DonVito, David Essex, John Hagood, Gretchen Hirschauer, Rodrick McElven, and Greg Most.

From the beginning this project has benefitted from the advice and encouragement of Joan García.

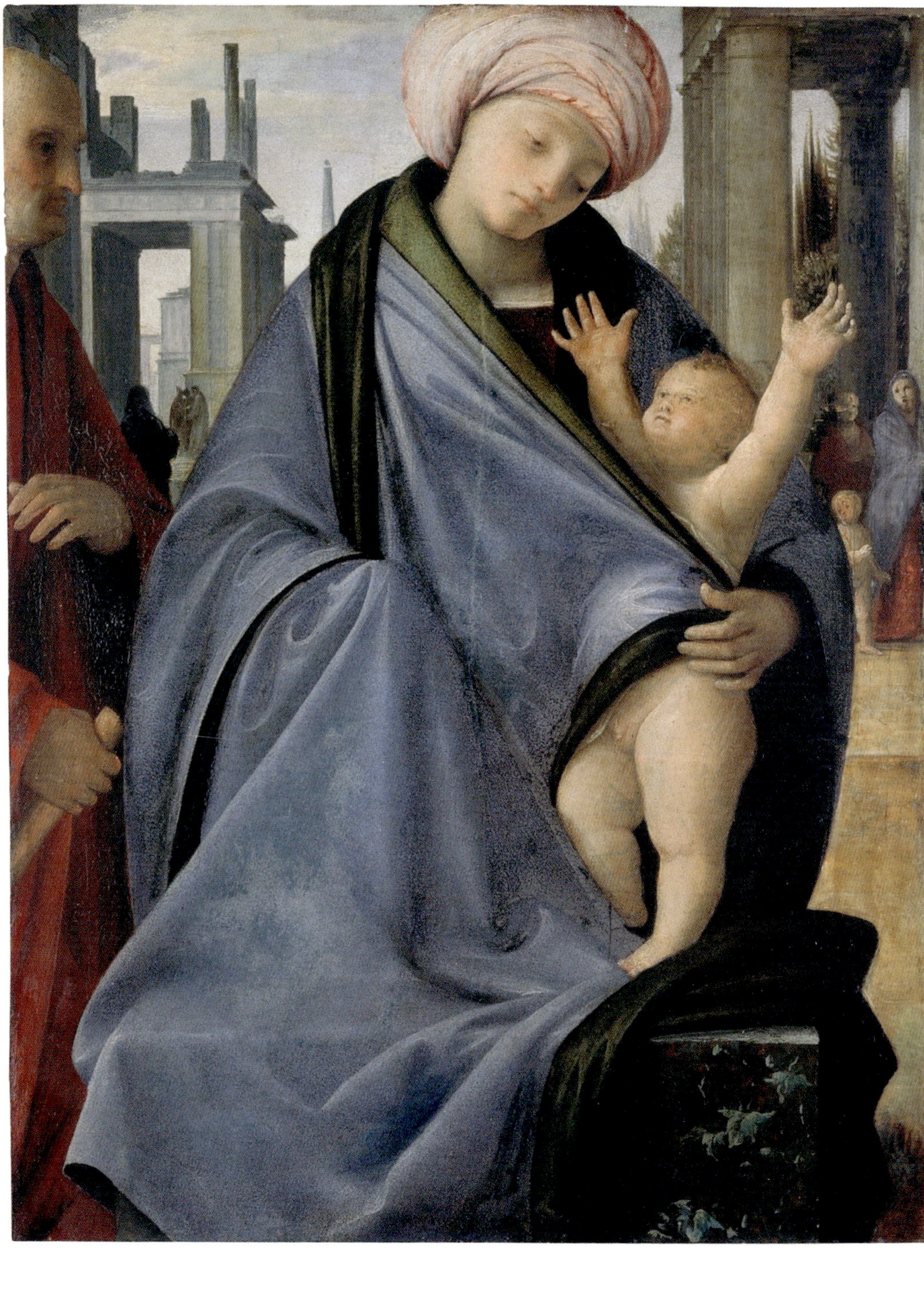

David Alan Brown

Overshadowed: Leonardo da Vinci and Bernardino Luini

This book revisits the idea that Leonardo da Vinci (1452–1519) was the essential inspiration for his younger contemporary Bernardino Luini (ca. 1480/85–1532). Instead of a broad notion of Leonardo's influence, however, the book offers a more complex understanding of the relation between the two artists, one that seeks to account for Luini's much-criticized lack of originality vis-à-vis the older master. In one artistic category in which Leonardo offered few models – devotional images of the Passion of Christ – Andrea Solario, himself influenced by Leonardo, had a decisive impact on Luini. Solario's influence complemented Leonardo's, enabling Luini to set a new standard for depicting a broad range of sacred subjects.

In later centuries Luini was esteemed as the pre-eminent early-sixteenth-century Lombard painter. Today he might have to vie for that honor with Bartolomeo Suardi, called Bramantino, whose style appears more modern than Luini's. Like his teacher Bramante, Bramantino (ca. 1465–1530) was a painter/architect who devised an artistic language all his own. Works, like his *Holy Family* (fig. 1) in the Pinacoteca di Brera, Milan, display a striking originality, in which quirky physiognomies, sweeping draperies, and striking architectural vistas all conform to a geometric order verging on abstraction. Not least for the subtle pictorial effects he achieved, Bramantino won the support of distinguished patrons, working briefly at the Vatican, designing a set of tapestries of the Months (Castello Sforzesco, Milan) for Gian Giacomo Trivulzio, and serving as court painter to Duke Francesco II Sforza. The singularity of his style, nevertheless, made his work an unsuitable model for devotional art on a wider scale, with the result that there are few copies of his paintings. Luini's more imitable works lack this sense of personality, but for that very reason they had a greater currency in Lombard art.

Fig. 1. Bartolomeo Suardi called Bramantino, *Holy Family*, Pinacoteca di Brera, Milan

Born Bernardino Scapi near the town of Luino (from which he took his name), Luini is first recorded in Milan in 1501, where he remained active for three decades until his death in 1532. Documents suggest that, at the age of about twenty, he had already embarked on his career as an artist. Few facts are known about his life, and he signed and dated relatively few pictures, so it is difficult to establish a chronology of his works. As far as we know, Luini was never Leonardo's pupil; he belongs, rather, to the second generation of Milanese painters influenced by him. Though he worked with equal facility in fresco and in oil on panel, Luini was a born muralist. As the most sought-after fresco painter in Lombardy, he completed numerous religious cycles for churches and convents in and around Milan, culminating in the frescoes of the life of Christ and the Virgin (1525) in the Sanctuary of Santa Maria dei Miracoli at Saronno and of the *Crucifixion with Scenes from the Passion* (1529) in the church of Santa Maria degli Angeli in Lugano. The detached fresco decorations he made for the town house and country villa of his patron Gerolamo Rabia are now divided between Milan, Berlin, and Washington, DC.

The problem of his relation to Leonardo runs like a leitmotif through the art-historical literature on Luini. Giorgio Vasari, touching on Luini in two of the artist biographies that make up his *Lives* (1568), does not link him with Leonardo, who, in Vasari's scheme, initiated the modern era in art.[2] Likewise, the Milanese art theorist Giovanni Paolo Lomazzo (1538–92) fails to connect the two.[3] For later critics, who associated the two artists, Leonardo's genius outshone Luini's talent except, briefly, in the seventeenth and nineteenth centuries, when the latter's reputation soared. The first to treat Leonardo and Luini as master and pupil was Cardinal Federico Borromeo, who, we shall find, owned works by both painters. A major protagonist of the Counter-Reformation in Milan, Borromeo was also the first to admire in Luini spiritual qualities that, for him, transcended Leonardo's mastery. By the end of the eighteenth century, knowledge about the two artists had progressed to the point where Luigi Lanzi, in a broad survey of Italian painting, could call Luini the master's closest and most celebrated follower, adding that some of his finest works were mistaken for Leonardo's.[4] Outside Italy, Johann David Passavant and Franz Kugler found in Luini's works a tender devotion and Alexis-François Rio, a religious zeal missing in Leonardo.[5] In England, meanwhile, Luini was not well known. Indeed, the leading Victorian art critic, John Ruskin (fig. 2), claimed to have discovered him. Luini was the main object of his study during the summer of 1862, when, accompanied by the pre-Raphaelite painter Edward Burne-Jones, Ruskin traveled to Milan. There he and his disciple made watercolor copies after Luini.[6] Ruskin's copies served for the chromolithographs, published by the Arundel Society, which introduced Luini to a wider public. Declaring him "ten times greater than Leonardo," Ruskin ranked Luini above the older master for the way he captured the "life-spirit" of art.[7] Later, he cogently observed that Luini never allowed his skill as an artist to "spoil the simplicity of his works or interfere with their direct appeal to the spectator."[8]

Ruskin's enthusiasm for Luini lifted him out from under Leonardo's shadow. No fewer than ten works by the artist were included in the Burlington Fine Arts Club exhibition of Milanese masters in 1898, and the following year the first and only English monograph on him appeared in print.[9] But the celebrity status Luini enjoyed with Ruskin and his readers was short-lived. Already in 1907, Bernard Berenson, in an essay entitled *North Italian Painters of the Renaissance*, denounced Luini and his colleagues as slavish imitators, whose work was of interest only as a reflection of Leonardo's.[10] Berenson dubbed Luini the "least intellectual of famous painters," meaning he lacked pictorial intelligence or the qualities of form, movement, and space that the author admired in other masters. Just as Ruskin's moralizing had elevated Luini, so Berenson's formalist approach demoted him to second-rate status. And his imitation of Leonardo was not just superficial. Luini was also unoriginal and repetitive, a charge that came with the use of photographs to reproduce artists' works in their totality. As the leading expert, responsible for bringing countless Italian paintings to America, Berenson's condemnation of Luini and the other members of Leonardo's circle proved decisive in relegating them once again

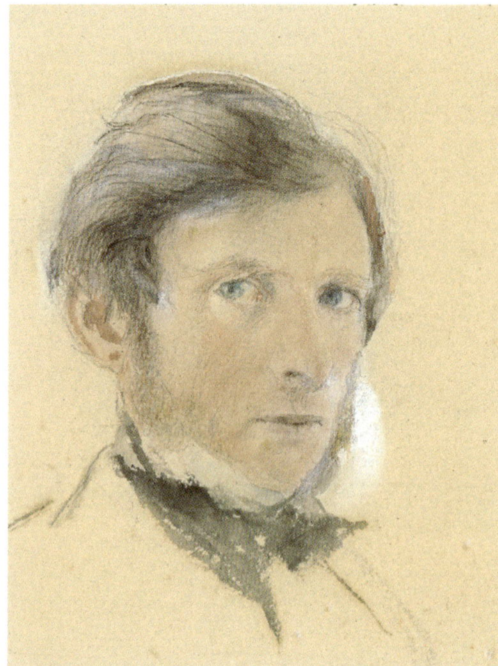

Fig. 2. John Ruskin, *Self-Portrait*, 1861, Morgan Library & Museum, New York

to obscurity. Even in Italy, Luini's reputation suffered, reaching a low ebb when the dean of Italian scholars Adolfo Venturi, in his multi-volume survey of Italian art, also berated Luini's lack of imagination.[11] He found the artist's work monotonous.

Splendid works by Luini are scattered throughout museums in Europe and America, but most of his production remains in and around Milan. Thus, it is not surprising that the first signs of a renewed interest in the artist lie in his native Lombardy. The Milanese architect-scholar Luca Beltrami's workhorse monograph of 1911 did not inspire further studies, and it was not until the mid-twentieth century that Luini's fortunes improved.[12] At that time what might be called a Lombard strategy for rescuing him from oblivion appeared in the form of another monograph, complete with catalogue, by Angela Ottino Della Chiesa.[13] Headquartered at the Brera, the single largest repository of his works, Ottino dissociated Luini from Leonardo to put him in a Lombard context. She saw the artist as a native son who reflected the character and spirit of the region in his art. No longer defining him, positively or negatively, in relation to Leonardo, Ottino's monograph became the go-to source for Luini. Maria Teresa Binaghi Olivari's patronage research also proved useful.[14] But it was two later projects, one an exhibition and the other a monograph, both with catalogues and both originating in Milan, that finally gave Luini the attention he deserves. The exhibition that Giovanni Agosti and Jacopo Stoppa organized at the Palazzo Reale in 2014 and the monograph that Brera Curator Cristina Quattrini brought out five years later offer an exemplary documentation of his work that is consistently cited here.[15] Though acknowledging Leonardo's importance for Luini, these scholars view his work as a distillation of many sources, Bramantino in particular.

Luini is not documented as Leonardo's pupil, and there is no evidence for any direct contact between them. Even so, he was certainly familiar with the master's work and aware of his presence in Milan. Born in Tuscany and regarded as a Florentine, Leonardo transferred his activity to the Lombard capital ca. 1482, where he worked as court artist and engineer to Duke Ludovico Sforza until the fall of his patron in 1499. It was during this first Milanese period that he created two of his most famous masterpieces – the *Last Supper* in the refectory of Santa Maria delle Grazie, and the so-called *Virgin of the Rocks*, known in two versions in Paris and London. After returning to Florence, Leonardo was called back to Milan by the new French rulers of the city in 1506/08. He and Luini overlapped there until 1513, when Leonardo left for Rome. From there he went to France, where he died in 1519. Leonardo's ability to combine art and science sets him apart from all but a few other artists. His investigations into optics, anatomy, botany, geology, and much else, when applied to art, formed what he called the "science of painting." Leonardo's goal as a painter was to recreate nature in all its variety. Such an ambitious program called for a lengthy, time-consuming process, resulting in an oeuvre of fewer than twenty extant pictures, some of which are unfinished owing to their creator's manifold interests and chronic inability to bring tasks to completion. Leonardo's works are also the product of endless revision. Conceptually dense, stylistically innovative, and painstakingly executed, they function on different levels and, to be properly understood, require careful observation and analysis. Though few in number, Leonardo's paintings exercised a profound influence on his contemporaries.

Luini's talents lay in a different direction: if Leonardo was a polymath, Luini was a painter pure and simple. To judge from his works, the younger artist shared neither Leonardo's wide-ranging intellectual interests nor his deep curiosity about the natural

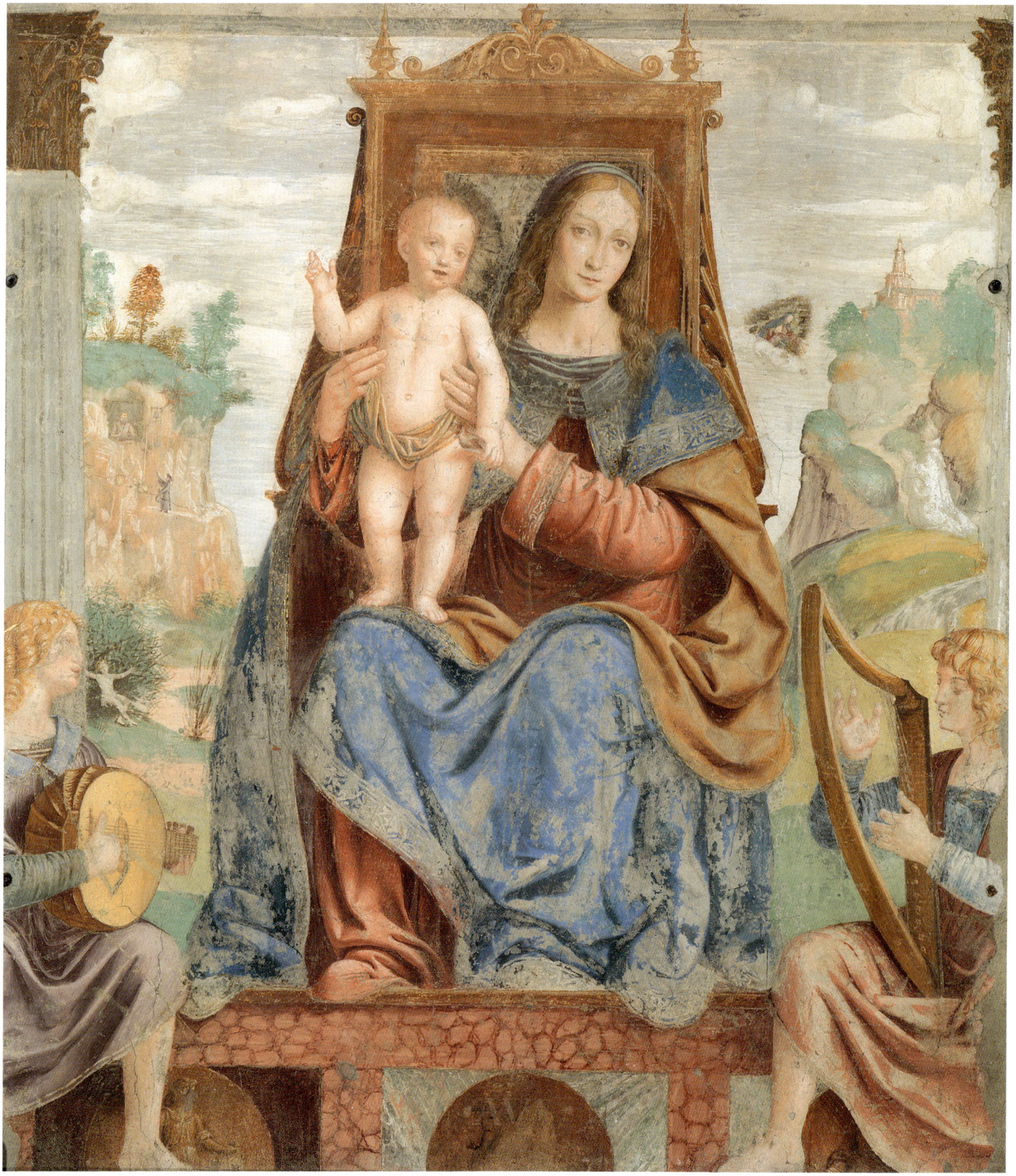

Fig 3. Bernardino Luini, *Virgin and Child Enthroned with Music-Making Angels*, Abbey of Chiaravalle (Milan)

world. But when it came to painting, Luini was more versatile and much more prolific, and, accustomed to fresco, he worked rapidly and efficiently. His facility and vast output are the antithesis of Leonardo's concentration on a few works of the utmost complexity. If for Leonardo each painting was a fresh start, the economy of Luini's production entailed the use of elements recombined from one picture to another. In this way Luini and his workshop produced a large quantity of art that is remarkably consistent in style and quality. He was a consummate professional whose fluency recommended him to a wide audience of worshipful spectators.

The artists' patrons differed in each case. The exceptional quality and rarity of Leonardo's paintings made them a prize for art lovers in Italy and beyond. He worked mainly for a culturally sophisticated clientele made up of rulers, including Ludovico Sforza's sister-in-law Isabella d'Este, the Borgia pope's son Cesare, the French governor of Milan Charles d'Amboise, successive kings of France Louis XII and Francis I, and the Medici pope's brother Giuliano – a veritable who's who of the time. Those who could not obtain works by the master visited his studio to report admiringly on their progress. Though he took on other commissions, *Mona Lisa*, for example, Leonardo was essentially a court artist in the mold of his predecessor Pisanello. Luini's audience was not limited to the political and cultural elite, and nothing suggests that he aspired to the rarefied social and intellectual circles in which Leonardo moved. His works appealed to all levels of society, from persons of wealth and position, like the aforementioned Gerolamo Rabia, to confraternities and religious institutions, and on to the nameless owners of his many Madonnas. He had the common touch. And with commissions pouring in from all sides, we can only admire his resourcefulness in adapting his art to the needs of his public.

Luini's first documented work is the *Virgin and Child Enthroned with Music-Making Angels* (fig. 3), datable to 1512, in the Cistercian Abbey of Chiaravalle near Milan.[16] Located at the head of the stairs leading to the monks' dormitory, the fresco is popularly known as the *Madonna della Buonanotte*. The execution of this work coincided with an event of great importance for the abbey, which played a role in the schismatic Council of Milan and Pisa. Religious life there is evoked in the landscape background, which depicts Saint Bernard, founder of the order, kneeling in prayer below a view of the abbey on the right, and Saint Benedict in penitence on the left. Rocky promontories sheltering episodes from the saints' lives flank the Virgin and Child, who look impassively out at the viewer. The strictly symmetrical composition extends to the musician angels, one playing a lute and the other a harp, at the base of the throne. The whole scene, viewed through a classical aedicule, is dominated by the Madonna whose voluminous draperies aim for an effect of monumentality.

Scholars have proposed a number of influences for the picture, but it is painted in a style betraying few, if any, direct connections with the work of other artists. The fresco harks back, instead, to the tradition of the leading fifteenth-century Lombard masters Foppa and Bergognone. Their individual styles differ, but the two shared an attitude toward nature and representation that privileged the world around them.[17] Luini clearly found this viewpoint congenial to his purpose. But he would also have found it conjoined in earlier Lombard painting with a staid figural language, and these two elements – naturalness and formality – seem to have been linked in his mind. Like his predecessors, Luini approached art as an extension of the real world, and, like them, his figures have a dignified demeanor. As a work of his early maturity, the Chiaravalle fresco demonstrates this continuity with the past, all

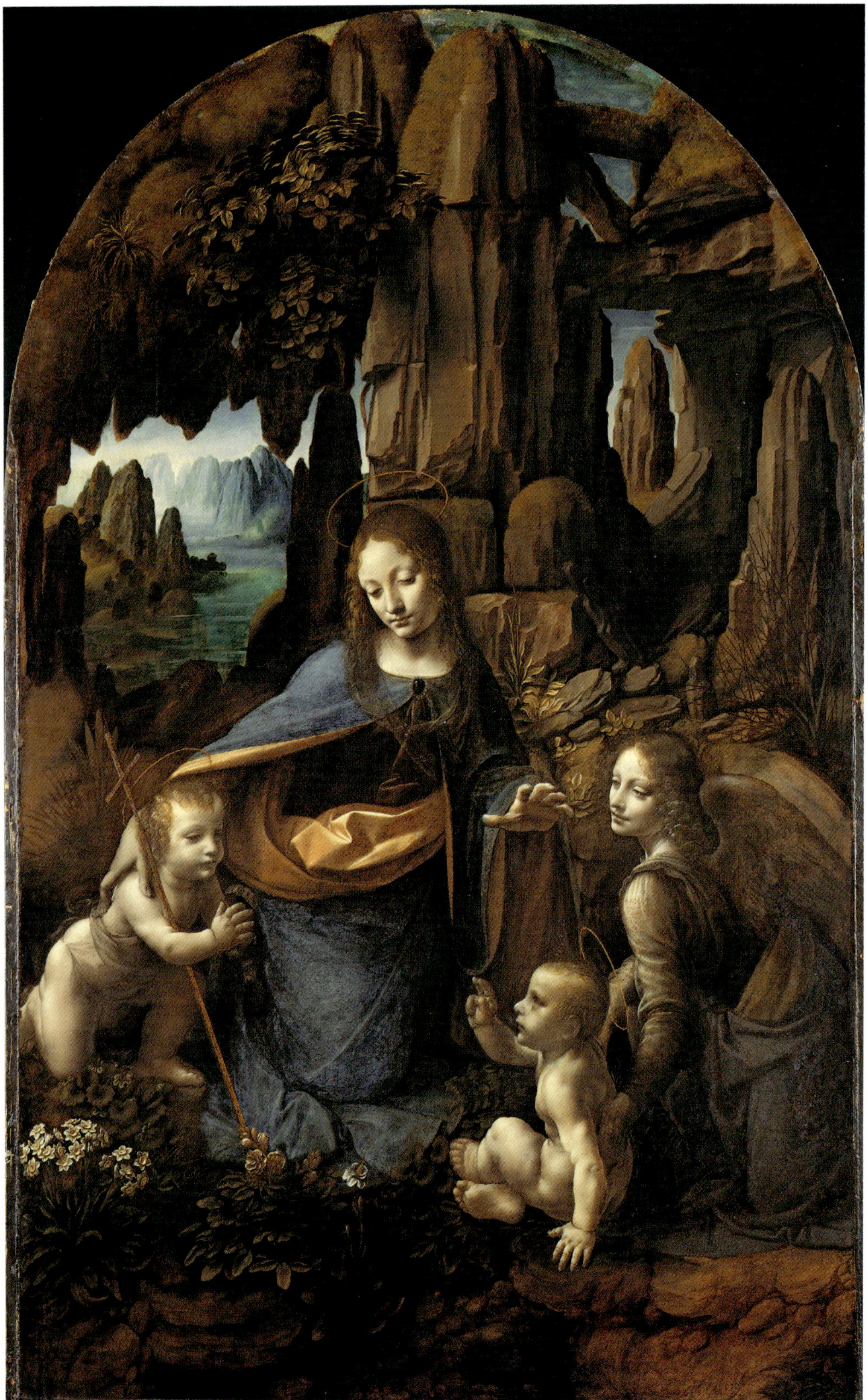

Figs. 4-4a. Leonardo da Vinci with Assistance, *Virgin of the Rocks*, whole and detail, The National Gallery, London

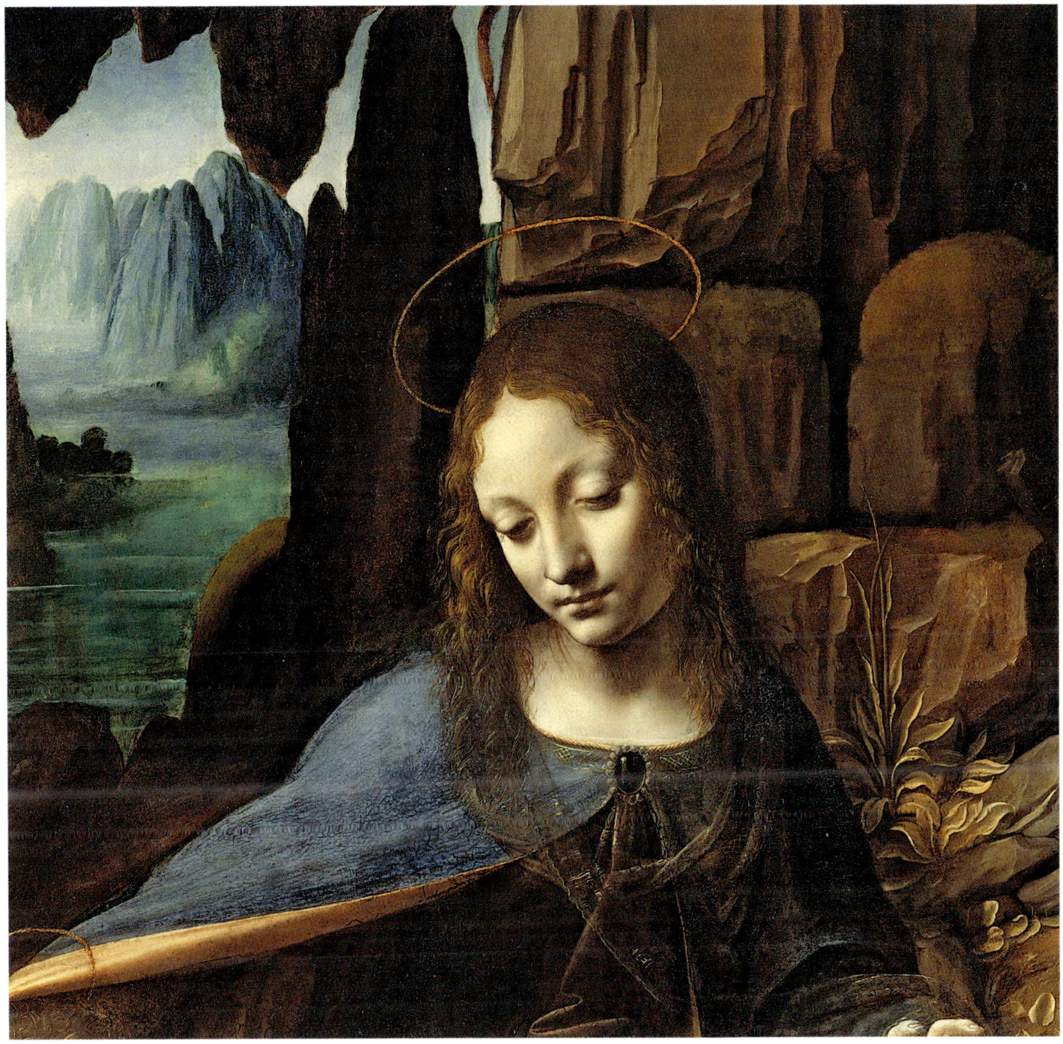

the while building on it. The facial type and imposing scale of the Virgin recall Leonardo, for example, if only in a general way.

The distance between Luini and Leonardo, at this moment, may be seen by comparing the latter's own treatment of the Madonna and Child with an Angel – the *Virgin of the Rocks* (figs. 4-4a), now in the National Gallery, London.[18] Newly arrived in Milan, Leonardo, together with the locals Ambrogio and Evangelista de Predis, agreed to paint an altarpiece for the chapel of the Confraternity of the Immaculate Conception in the church of San Francesco Grande. The agreement between the confraternity and the artists, dated April 25, 1483, stipulated a series of paintings to join an ensemble of already sculpted figures and reliefs. The series was meant to include a central panel of the Virgin and Child accompanied by prophets and angels and subsidiary panels again with angels. The contract also called for a lavish display of gold in the costumes, and the artists were to paint and gild the frame and the sculptural decoration as well. Clearly, the altarpiece envisaged by the patrons was traditional in form and content. Their dismay may well be imagined when Leonardo, ignoring the terms of the contract, produced the first version of the *Virgin of the Rocks* now in the

Fig. 5. Bernardino Luini, *Virgin and Child with the Infant Saint John the Baptist*, The National Gallery, London

Louvre. Completed between 1483 and 1486, the altarpiece essentially represents a continuity with his previous Florentine practice. Depicting an apocryphal meeting between the infants Christ and Saint John the Baptist in the wilderness, the central panel for the confraternity's *ancona* must have seemed disconcerting, not only for the novel pyramidal grouping of the figures in a dark, cavernous setting, but also for the emphasis placed on Florence's patron saint. Not surprisingly, therefore, when Leonardo and Ambrogio requested an additional sum for the picture, the confraternity refused. The artists then seem to have withheld the painting in order to dispose of it elsewhere, obliging them to come up with a second version of the composition, the one now in London, to satisfy the commission.

As an intellectual enterprise, Leonardo's painting has prompted numerous scholarly interpretations. But whether the members of the confraternity grasped the complex Marian symbolism of the picture is open to question. Indeed, scholars still dispute its meaning. But the work found wanting by the confraternity was apparently sought by another, unnamed client, possibly Ludovico Sforza, whom the artists asked to intervene in the dispute. In their appeal they claimed that the members of the confraternity were unqualified to decide such matters ("the blind cannot judge colors").[19] Acting as arbiter, the duke would surely award them the compensation they deserved for creating a masterpiece like nothing else in Lombard art. There were patrons, after all, for whom the spiritual content of a work did not exclude an appreciation of its beauty.

Documents indicate that the London painting, known to have come from San Francesco Grande, was begun in the 1490s and brought to its present near-complete state between 1506 and 1508, when Leonardo returned to French-occupied Milan. It remained in the church for centuries until the confraternity was dissolved and the painting was sold. While critics agree that the Louvre picture is entirely autograph, the London *Virgin of the Rocks* is widely regarded as a work jointly executed by Leonardo and one or more assistants.[20] Technical investigation, preceding the treatment of the painting in 2010 failed to resolve this issue. But it did reveal the existence of an underdrawing for a wholly different grouping of the figures, minus the Baptist, suggesting that Leonardo first proposed another composition as a substitute for the confraternity's picture, then opted to supply a copy instead. The artist's monochrome underpainting also emerged. Partly visible on the surface, the underpainting largely accounts for the grayish flesh tones of the figures and lends the picture its tonal unity.[21]

As the confraternity that commissioned the altarpiece was dedicated to the Immaculate Conception, it has been claimed that Leonardo made various changes in the London picture to conform to their wishes. Though scholarly attention has focused on the re-conception of the angel – Leonardo omitted his pointing gesture and outward glance – small but significant adjustments to all the figures lend them a greater stature. They are larger in scale in relation to the picture area, and their draperies loop around to link them together. The image of the Virgin especially has gained in grandeur. Her features, while still recalling those of her counterpart in Paris, have been modified: no longer the young mother, she is more serious and introspective, like the angel. The most important change, however, has to do with Leonardo's use of chiaroscuro. By contrast to the illumination in the Louvre picture, the light here models forms in strong contrasts of light and shade, with areas of dense shadow subduing color. The sharply focused fall of light from the upper left creates a powerful sense of *rilievo*, or three-dimensionality, which lends the protagonists, set off against the dark background, an almost sculptural quality. At

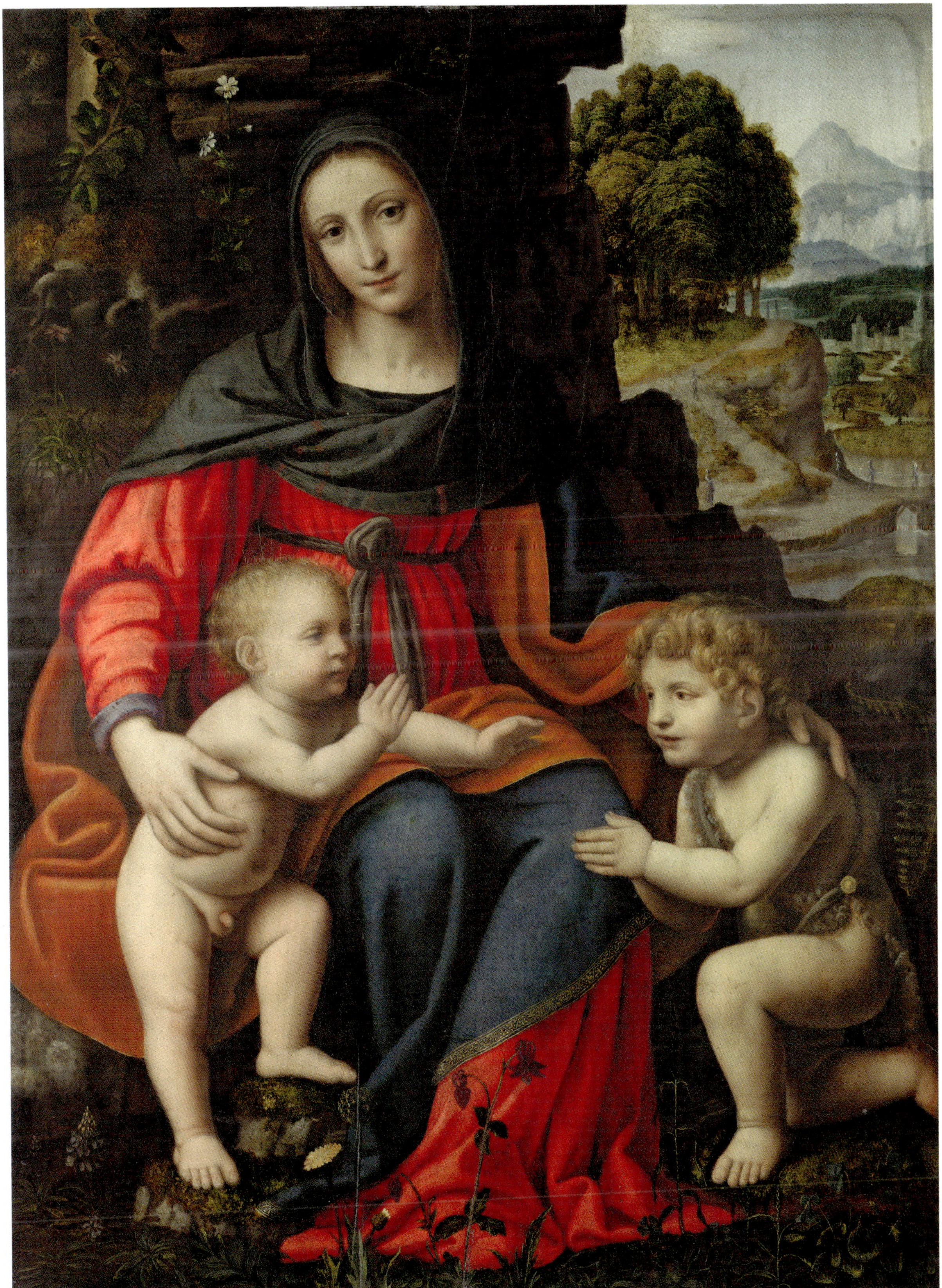

the same time the modeling of the figures displays an extraordinary sensitivity to tonal values, expressed in extremely fine gradations of shading. Both aspects – the light-dark contrasts and the gradation of tones – may well reflect Leonardo's scientific investigations of light and shadow. Many pertinent observations are recorded in the master's notebooks A and C, dating to the early 1490s, when he undertook the revision of the *Virgin of the Rocks*.[22]

Coming after Leonardo's masterpiece, Luini's considerably smaller panel of the *Virgin and Child with the Infant Saint John the Baptist* (fig. 5), also in the National Gallery, makes a disappointing impression.[23] In this early work, datable to around 1510, the younger artist grafted elements from Leonardo's altarpiece onto the plainspoken Lombard naturalism he had inherited. In Luini's much simplified version of his prototype, the figure group is inverted and brought closer to the picture plane. The Virgin is shown seated, rather than kneeling, beside the two holy infants, with Christ on the left and John the Baptist on the right. Her facial type and the tilt of her head are borrowed from Leonardo, but not her expression. With barely a hint of a smile, she looks directly out at the viewer as if to include him or her in the picture. Also departing from Leonardo's example, the Virgin's hair is modestly veiled and her garments brightly colored. Finally, if the infants in the *Virgin of the Rocks* were sometimes confused (as suggested by the addition of the Baptist's cross-staff in the London version), Luini sought to clarify their identities. He depicts the older, larger, curly-headed figure of John wearing his traditional camel skin and, to differentiate them further, has Christ stand to welcome the Baptist kneeling before him. The meeting of the infant Christ and his cousin in the desert is not recorded in the Bible, but goes back to a *Vita* of Saint John attributed to the Dominican friar Domenico Cavalca.[24] It was frequently represented in fifteenth-century Florentine art. Also a favorite of Luini's, the popularity of the theme in Lombardy after 1500 was undoubtedly due to Leonardo's example.

Leonardo's protagonists have an air of mystery, and so does the landscape around them. The grotto may have Immaculist overtones, but it can only have seemed strange and unsettling to the members of the confraternity, who, looking at the picture, were transported to another realm. The landscape is the product of Leonardo's *fantasia*, or imagination, and yet it is made to appear real by his understanding of the natural world. As rendered by an assistant, perhaps, the flora dotting the foreground and the rock formations are not so carefully observed as in the Louvre version, but they still convey a sense of actuality thanks to the light and shadow in which they are immersed. While Leonardo's setting seems remote, Luini's, by contrast, evokes the everyday world of the viewer. The mysterious grotto in the *Virgin of the Rocks* has here been reduced to a rocky backdrop against which the characters are illuminated in the clear light of day. Behind, tiny figures move along a path traversing a bluff, topped by leafy green trees, overlooking a valley with a town before distant blue mountains. These are landscape conventions employed by Luini to familiarize the scene. In the same way the plants surrounding the figures are native to northern Italy and have widely understood symbolic meanings. The London painting shows how Luini initially responded to the *Virgin of the Rocks* when it was new. Though doubtless aware of Leonardo's innovations, he applied them only sparingly in his own work. Taking over what he needed to communicate a straightforward spiritual content and no more, he succeeded in demystifying Leonardo's achievement. But at what cost? The stiff, expressionless figures seem inert by comparison, particularly the open-faced Virgin, who lacks the sense of inner life animating all of Leonardo's creations. In Luini's hands the extreme has become commonplace.

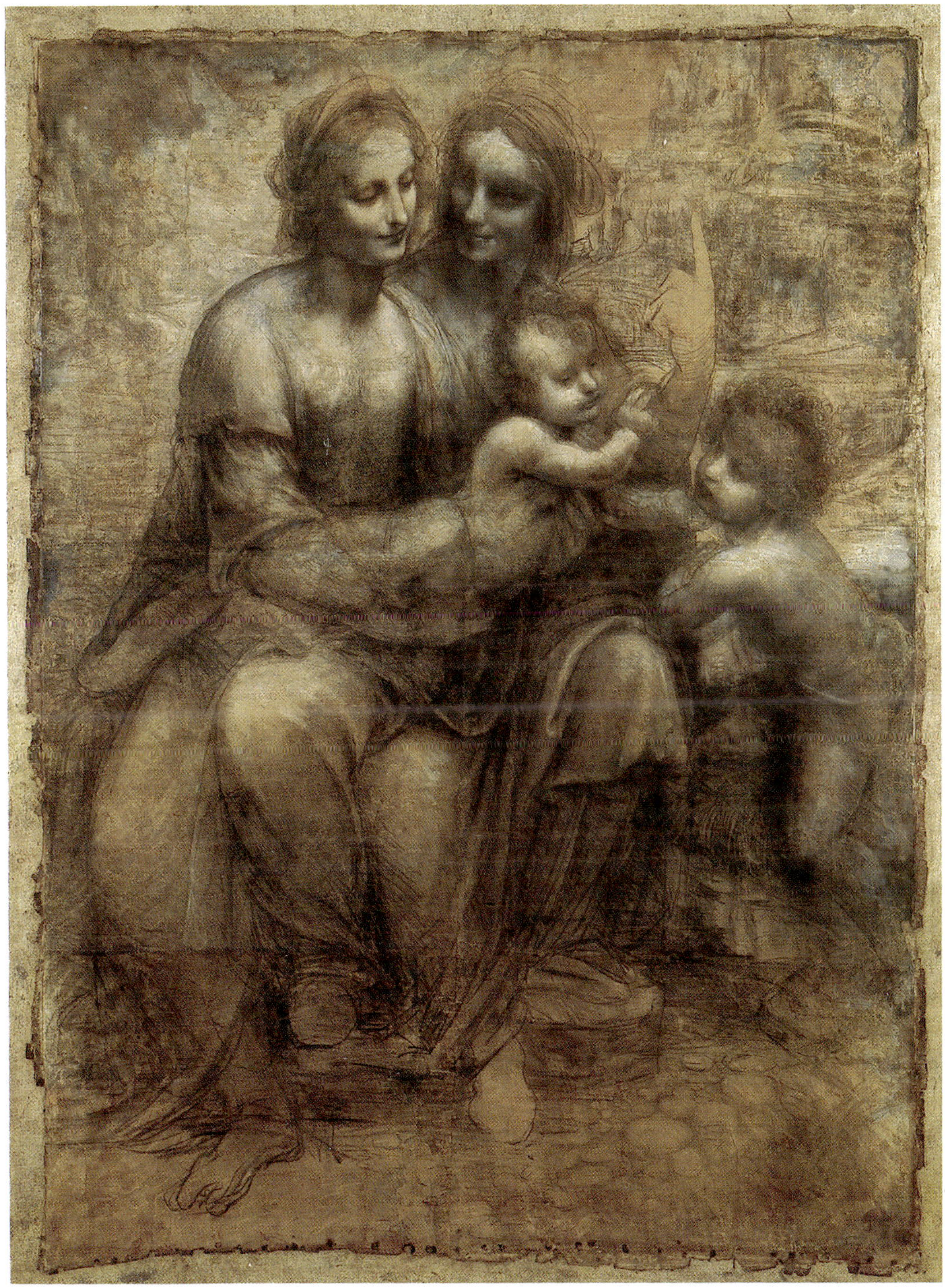

Fig. 6. Leonardo da Vinci, *Virgin and Child with Saint Anne and the Infant Saint John the Baptist*, The National Gallery, London

While the *Virgin of the Rocks* remained unfinished, Leonardo undertook a similar composition, in which the Virgin's mother Saint Anne substitutes for the angel. This work, also in the National Gallery, is a cartoon (fig. 6), or full-scale preparatory drawing, for a never-executed altarpiece.[25] The outlines of the cartoon are not pricked for transfer from paper to panel, giving the drawing the character of an independent work of art. Leonardo's bold use of charcoal and black chalk with white heightening on eight sheets of paper glued together creates a compelling image, even if some details, like the hands and feet of the female figures and the landscape, are not fully defined. The artist began to develop the theme of the Virgin and Child with Saint Anne and the infant Saint John the Baptist after returning to Florence in 1500, and it was only after numerous changes in design that the cartoon came into being. Evidence of his creative process is a rapid pen-and-ink sketch of the same group (fig. 7) in the British Museum, London.[26] Here and in other freely drawn sketches, Leonardo experimented with different solutions to compositional problems. The overdrawn figures on the sheet are barely legible and would doubtless have puzzled the master's Milanese pupils and followers, who turned to the cartoon and other more finished works for guidance and inspiration.

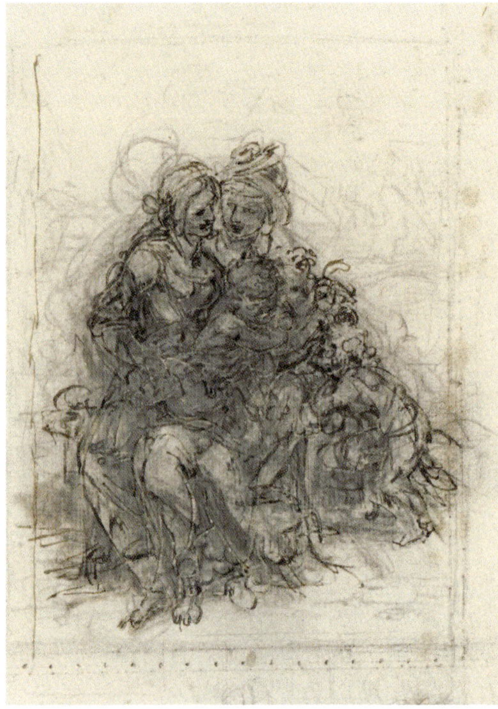

Fig. 7. Leonardo da Vinci, *Virgin and Child with Saint Anne and the Infant Baptist*, detail, Department of Prints and Drawings, The British Museum, London

As in the *Virgin of the Rocks*, the compositional structure of the cartoon is a pyramid with the figures positioned on a rocky ledge before a mountainous landscape background. Saint Anne, symbolizing the Incarnation, turns to gaze lovingly at her daughter and points upwards to indicate the deeper spiritual meaning of the event as a foreshadowing of Christ's Passion. With Anne acting as a central axis, the near-life-size figures are arranged along a diagonal leading from the Virgin to the Baptist. Their complex poses reflect what Leonardo called the "motions of the mind" (*moti*), or body movements appropriate to the mental states of his subjects. Seated sideways on her mother's right thigh, the Virgin turns to hold out the infant Christ, while he swivels in her arms to bless the curly-headed Baptist approaching from the right. The way the characters are combined in a single cohesive group has a pronounced sculptural quality.[27] And their exceedingly graceful demeanor gives them the air of superior beings enacting a high-stakes drama, the effect of which is heightened by Leonardo's chiaroscuro modeling. But the figures' compressed energy comes with a drawback: the result does not appear spontaneous or natural. Even today, the juxtaposed heads and legs of the two females are confusing: they look like sisters, and the Virgin's bent knee might be mistaken for Anne's right leg. Drawing on his brainstorming sketches, Leonardo has achieved the maximum *contrapposto*, but the cartoon reads more like a feat of figural dynamics than a religious image whose form and content are readily accessible to the viewer.

The difficulties of the cartoon have been ironed out in Leonardo's painting of the *Virgin and Child with Saint Anne and a Lamb* (fig. 8) in the Louvre.[28] On a wood panel somewhat smaller than the cartoon, the picture had a long gestation: Leonardo began it during his second Florentine period, carried it further in Milan from 1508 to 1513, and left it unfinished at his death in 1519. In Milan, he was said to be working on "two paintings of Our Lady of different sizes" for Louis XII,

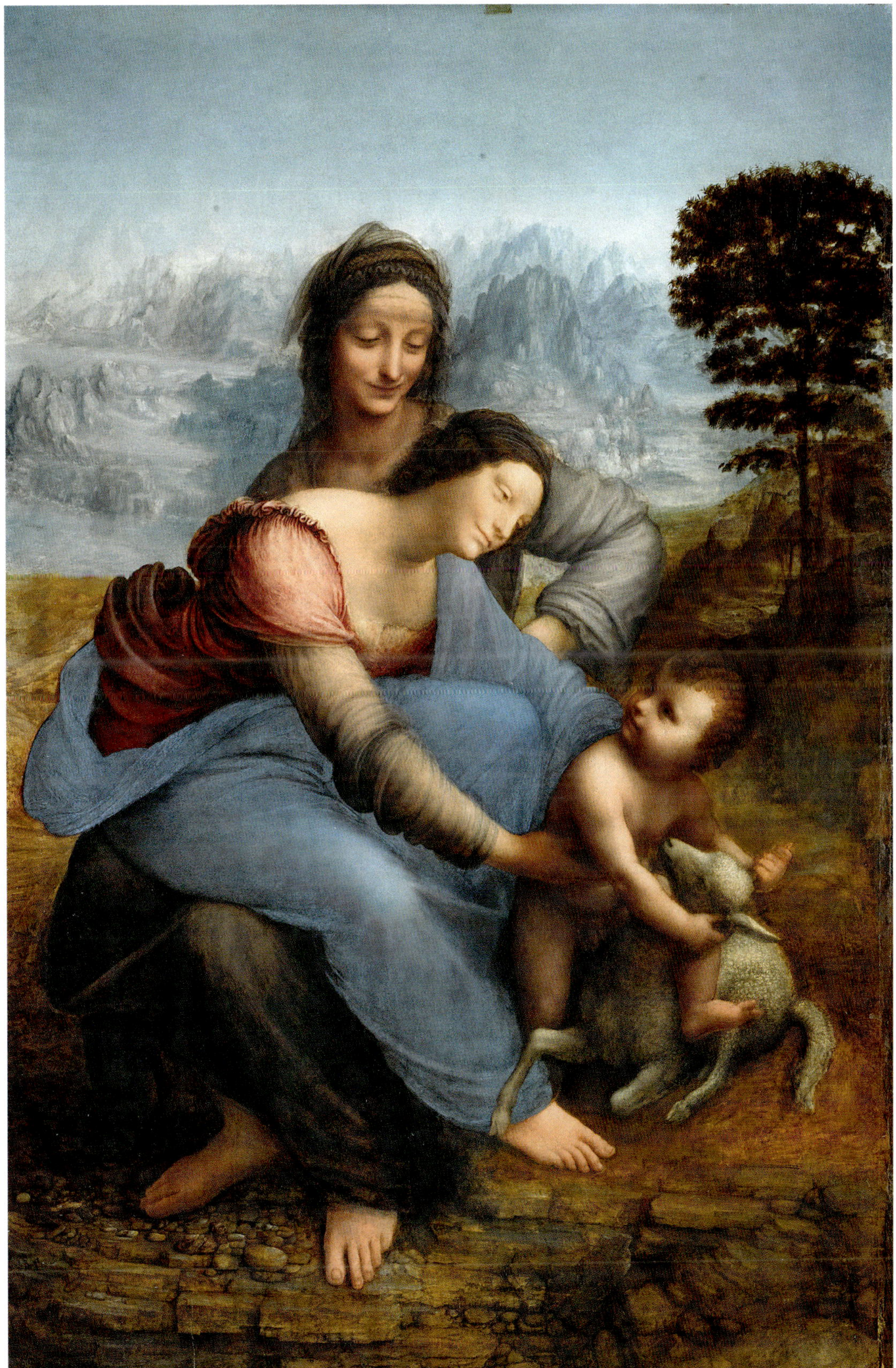

Fig. 8. Leonardo da Vinci, *Virgin and Child with Saint Anne and a Lamb*, Musée du Louvre, Paris

and critics agree that the *Saint Anne*, as it is called, might be one of these.[29] The painting features the same beautifully expressive cast of characters as the cartoon, except for the infant Baptist whose place is taken by his attribute, the sacrificial lamb. As in the cartoon, a wide variety of movements is combined within a single group, but here Leonardo overcomes the precarious equilibrium of that work by turning the females in different directions. In the center Anne looks down smiling at the Virgin, who, seated on her lap, bends over to restrain the Child attempting to mount the lamb. His pose mimics hers, as he grasps the lamb by the ears and, turning backward, looks fondly at his mother as if to seek her reassurance or approval. The motif appears playful but is deadly serious, as Christ's action signals his acceptance of his tragic fate.

Along with posture adjustments, the addition of color helps to clarify the figure arrangement in the Louvre picture. The Virgin's rose-red dress and light blue robe, draped over her legs, stand out against the subdued grayish tones of Saint Anne's garments. Leonardo has taken the figures out of the shadows, with the accent on his other signature pictorial device of *sfumato*. Technical studies have shown that he achieved this softening or blurring of contours by a slow, deliberative process of layer upon layer of thinly pigmented glazes and extremely fine brushwork. The change to a more suffused light and a softer, more atmospheric rendering of forms also affects the landscape background, where a vast mountain range, bathed in a bluish haze, extends behind the figures. This strange, fantastical panorama, based on Leonardo's geological studies, betrays no trace of human habitation or presence. It is a place apart.

The London cartoon and the Louvre painting now joined the *Virgin of the Rocks* (fig. 4) as Luini's major sources of inspiration. The artist's fresco of the *Virgin and Child with the Infant Saint John the Baptist and a Lamb* (fig. 9), on long-term loan from the Brera to the Museo Nazionale della Scienza e della Tecnologia, Milan, marks an advance in his approach to Leonardo.[30] If Luini's earlier adaptation of the altarpiece in San Francesco Grande might be called simplistic, the Milan picture shows a better understanding of how he could employ Leonardo's models in his own work. Datable to the second half of the 1510s, the fresco comes from the Milanese "ospizio," or residence, of the monks of the Certosa di Pavia, located next to the church of San Michele alla Chiusa. The work was detached from the wall on which it was painted, transferred to canvas, and subsequently restored in 1990/91. Since fresco dries quickly and bonds with the wall, Leonardo, working slowly and deliberately, never adopted this technique for mural painting. Luini, by contrast, painted simply and directly, adding details to the surface when the plaster was dry. Fresco was incapable of creating saturated dark tones, and his light colorful palette appears well suited to the outdoor setting of his picture.

When he left Milan for Rome in the autumn of 1513, Leonardo evidently took the two Saint Anne depictions with him, obliging Luini to rely on his memory of the cartoon and the painting he had apparently seen in the master's studio. The subject of Luini's picture is, again, the encounter of the Holy Family with the Infant Saint John on the Return from the Flight into Egypt. His debt to Leonardo is for the figures, organized in a diagonal toward the lower right. Luini similarly places his protagonists on a rocky ledge close to the picture plane and adds the bearded Joseph, dressed, like the Virgin, in mauve and golden yellow, in the background. This arrangement is the result of deconstructing the cartoon and the painting – a process that argues for a growing skill in the artist's use of sources. The first step was to eliminate Saint Anne, who was not part of Luini's conception. Another

Fig. 9. Bernardino Luini, *Virgin and Child with the Infant Saint John the Baptist and a Lamb*, Pinacoteca di Brera on loan to the Museo Nazionale della Scienza e della Tecnologia, Milan

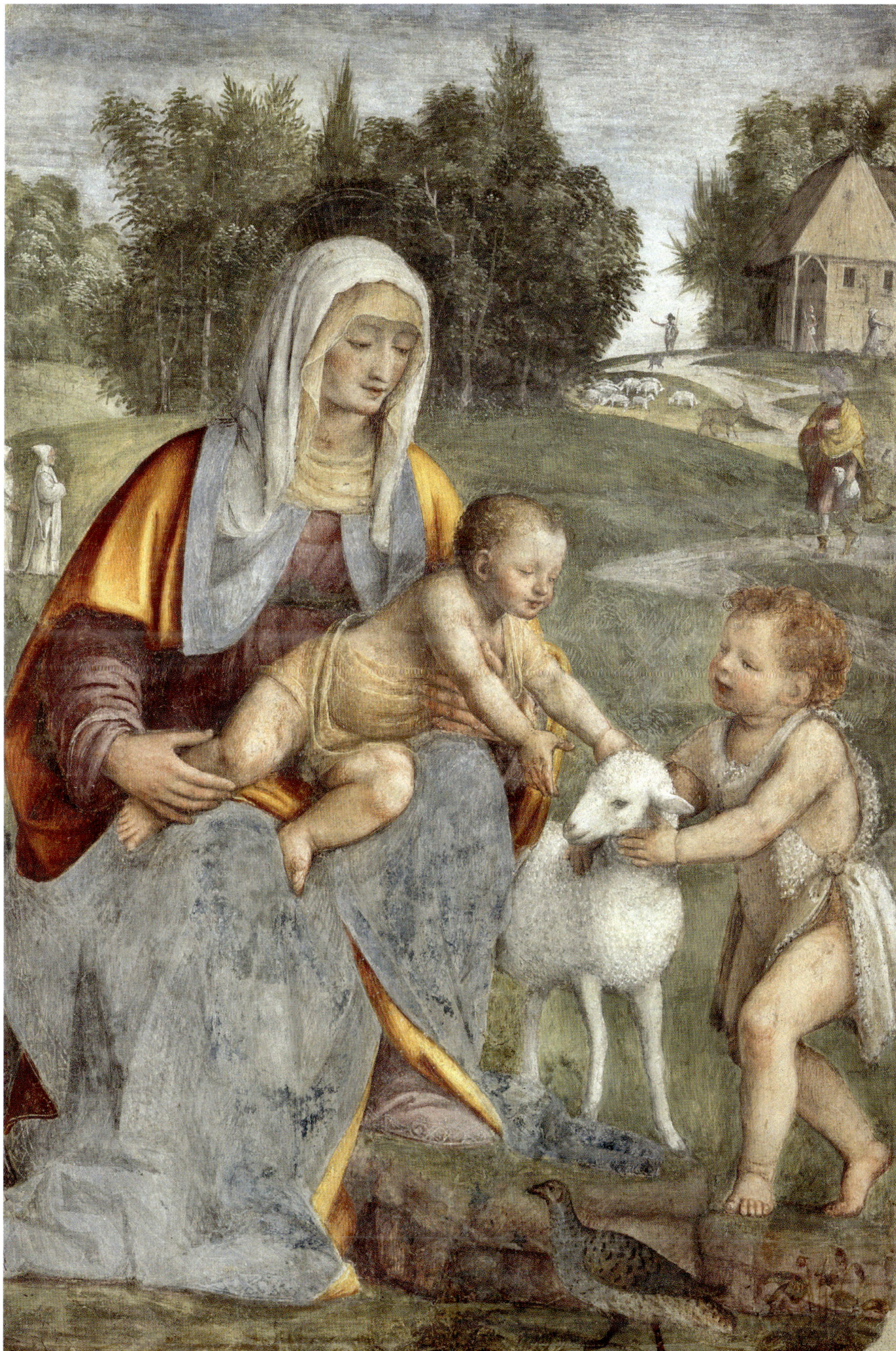

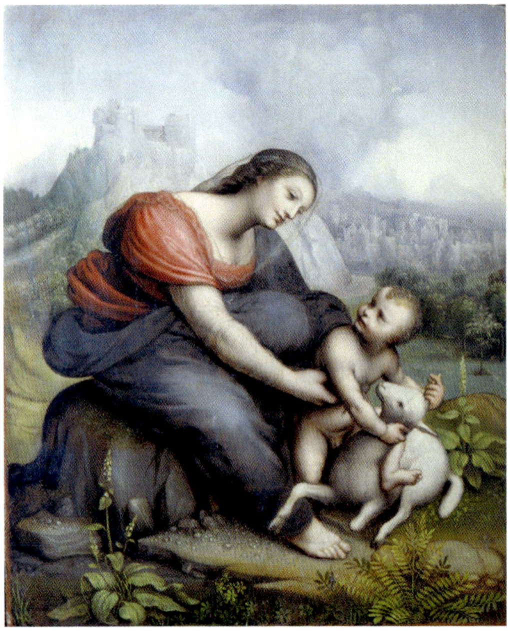

Fig. 10. Cesare da Sesto, *Virgin and Child with a Lamb*, Museo Poldi Pezzoli, Milan

Milanese follower of Leonardo's named Cesare da Sesto also omitted her figure in his version (fig. 10) of the Louvre panel in the Museo Poldi Pezzoli, Milan.[31] But whereas Cesare exactly copied Leonardo's other characters, Luini freely adapted them to suit his purpose. Combining his models, Luini includes both the infant Baptist and the lamb in one and the same picture.[32] In his formulation, the Virgin, seated upright, holds the Child, who reaches out eagerly for the lamb steadied by the little Saint John. Leonardo typically showed the lamb bending under the Child's weight, whereas Luini has the animal simply wait to be straddled. Throughout the principal group, the younger artist avoids Leonardo's contrapposto in favor of actions that appear artless and unaffected. And there is no rapturous exchange of glances.

The lighthearted mood of Luini's figures extends to the landscape background. In his source (fig. 8), the eerily deserted scene is devoid of vegetation except for a lone tree. Luini's landscape evokes the Lombard countryside. A grove of trees serves as a foil for the Virgin's head, while, within walking distance, verdant hills slope upwards to a farmhouse. Nearby is a flock of sheep, which account, so to speak, for the sacrificial lamb. Meanwhile Joseph approaches, carrying a knapsack with provisions for the Holy Family on their journey. Luini's painting thus offers a charming vignette whose devotional aspect – what raises it above the ordinary – is not any heightened emotionality of the figures but specific elements, like the haloes, the Virgin's pious head covering, and the partridge and the columbine, symbolizing the Passion, in the lower right. The pair of monks traversing the landscape, on the left, refers to Luini's patrons, the Carthusians, who, thanks to their inclusion, could see themselves in his work.

In this and other works from the decade following the Chiaravalle fresco, Luini sought to forge a down-to-earth devotional style that would translate Leonardo's figural language into a Lombard idiom grounded in reality as it is commonly perceived. In doing so, the artist popularized Leonardo's manner, purging it of complexities in favor of a style that imbues his subjects with a sense of the everyday. Of course, there are many devotional styles that vary according to the individual artist and the time and place in which he worked, and Luini is no exception. But his style does not draw attention to itself or its creator. By contrast to Leonardo's conspicuous artistry, Luini's sacred figures appear frank and unaffected. What an earlier generation of critics viewed as inability or lack of imagination we can see as a mode of expression perfectly suited to the artist's goal of communicating a straightforward religious content in his pictures. His style spoke to a wide swath of worshippers, from churchmen to ordinary Lombards intent on their devotions.

Leonardo painted few pictures to serve as models for other artists. Another factor limiting his influence was the small number of religious subjects he treated, mostly the Virgin and Child, with or without other figures,

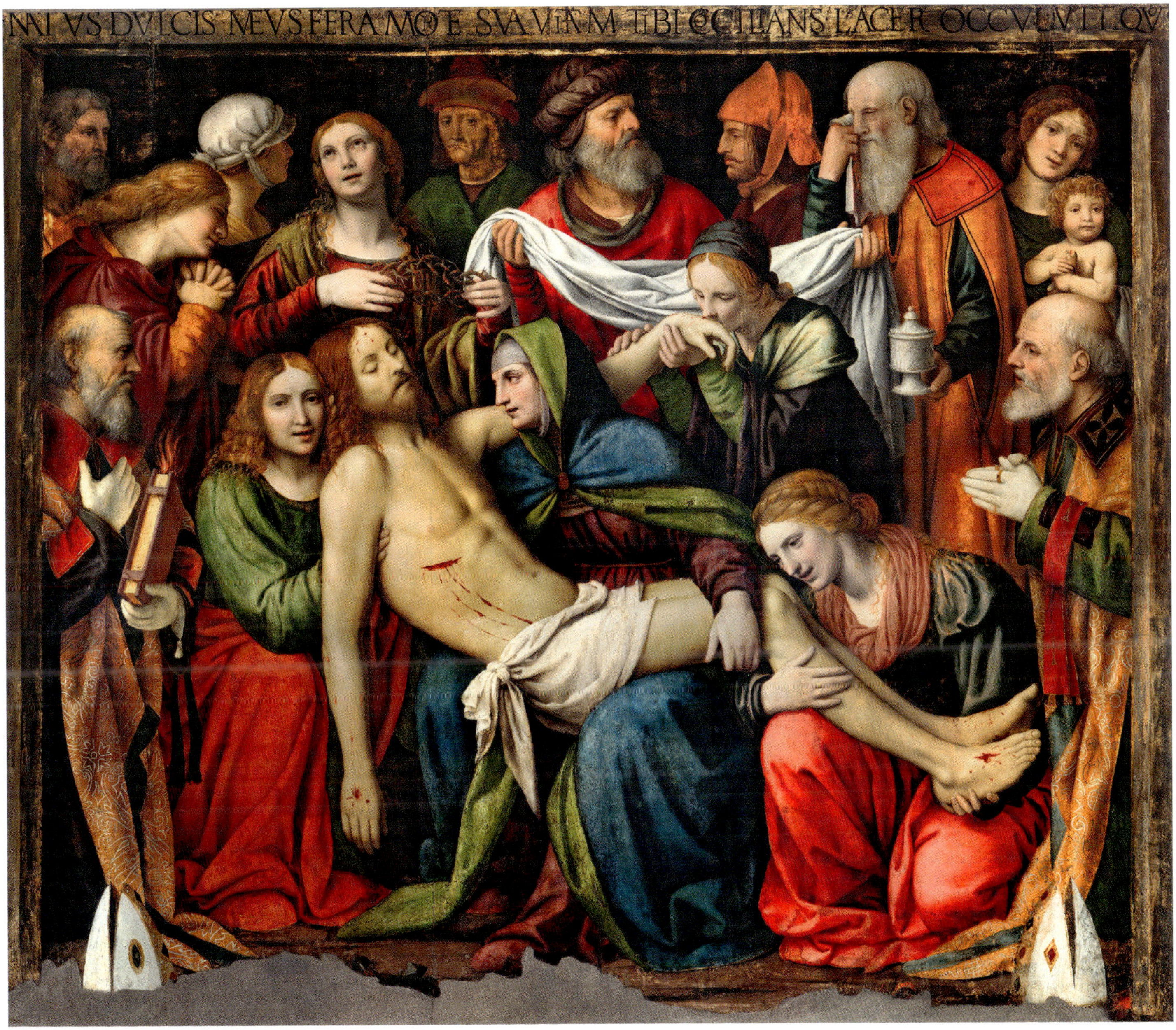

Fig. 11. Bernardino Luini, *Lamentation over the Dead Christ*, Cappella del Santissimo Sacramento, San Giorgio al Palazzo, Milan

but no scenes from Christ's Passion, except for the *Last Supper* and a half-length depiction of Christ Carrying the Cross, which may have reached the stage of a cartoon.[33] Artists in Milan, as elsewhere, were obliged, nevertheless, to depict all kinds of devotional themes, and those relating to the Passion required an emotional range beyond the quietude of Luini's Madonnas. The sobriety of the artist's earlier works was simply inadequate to express the pathos of Christ's suffering and death on the Cross. Because the account of the Passion in the Gospels was rather meager, a religious movement grew up, spearheaded by prayer manuals and devotional tracts like the *Meditations on the Life of Christ* by an anonymous Franciscan known as the pseudo-Bonaventura or Thomas à Kempis's *Imitation of Christ*. Abridged and translated, these and other medieval texts became enormously popular. Vivid new scenes focused on Christ's humanity, rather than his divinity, with the faithful urged to empathize with his plight. The climate created by the texts, then, gave rise to a new class of visual images that facilitated private devotion by creating a more intimate relation between Christ and the worshipper.

Luini's older contemporary Andrea Solario (ca. 1465–1524) excelled in this field. The painting specialist in a Lombard family of sculptors and architects, Solario was briefly active in Venice before returning to work for the new French rulers of Milan. His most important commission involved a fresco decoration for Cardinal Georges d'Amboise, destroyed during the French Revolution. Solario's contribution to the development of devotional art in Lombardy was of fundamental importance for Luini. Indeed, their works in this vein have often been confused. In a series of half-length depictions of the Ecce Homo, Christ Carrying the Cross, and Salome with the Head of the Baptist, Solario interpreted iconographic types in terms of Leonardo's pictorial language of pose, gesture and expression.[34] The artist's *Ecce Homo* (fig. 12) in the Ashmolean Museum, Oxford, typifies his approach.[35] Isolated from a narrative context, the tightly arranged figures of Christ and his adversaries stand out against a dark background. The dramatic close-up focuses on their actions and emotions with the goal of arousing pity or compassion in the viewer.

Inspired by Leonardo, Solario's handling of devotional themes, in turn, influenced the style and imagery of Luini's half-length compositions. And it affected one of his altarpieces as well. The *Lamentation over the Dead Christ* (fig. 11) that Luini painted for the chapel of the Santissimo Sacramento in the church of San Giorgio al Palazzo, Milan, marks a breakthrough in his career.[36] Still in situ in a shallow chapel on the right side of the nave, this squarish panel forms the centerpiece of a decorative cycle the artist completed in 1516 for

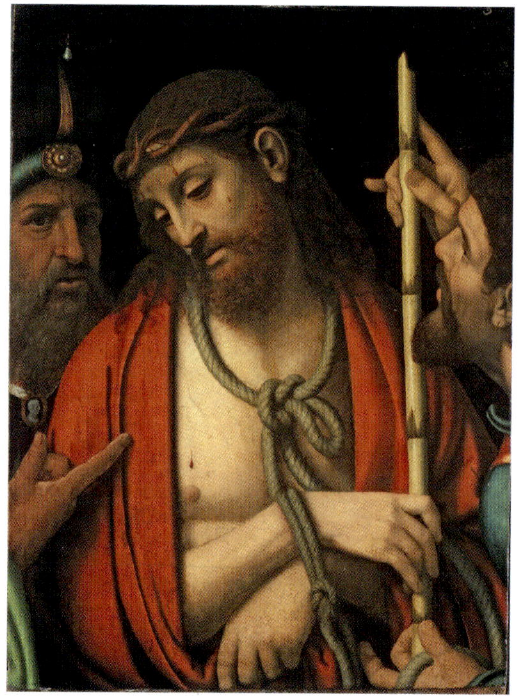

Fig. 12. Andrea Solario, *Ecce Homo*, Ashmolean Museum, Oxford

Luca Terzaghi, chancellor of the Confraternity of the Santissimo Sacramento headquartered in the church. The decoration consists of two large panels with the *Flagellation* and the *Ecce Homo* on the side walls, the *Lamentation* over the altar, and the lunette-shaped *Crowning with Thorns* beneath an illusionistic fresco of the *Crucifixion* on the vault. The light source is consistent throughout, but the figure scale and settings differ so the overall effect, while suggesting recession into depth, is not strictly unified.

The perspectival scheme, in any case, leads to the *Lamentation*, where the mourners grieving over the dead Christ fill the available space. The protagonists – the Virgin and the youthful Saint John the Evangelist supporting Christ's body on her lap; Mary Magdalene at his feet; three holy women, one holding the crown of thorns; and Nicodemus and Joseph of Arimathea, displaying the shroud and ointment jar of his burial – are life-size, establishing a connection with the viewer. Flanking the central group are two bishop saints, kneeling in profile, who have been identified as Augustine, on the left, and Ambrose, on the right. They witness the event, as we do, while John, looking out, meets the viewer's glance and draws him or her into the picture. Behind the principal figures are the heads of several bystanders unaware of the action taking place in the foreground. Luini's composition, packed with figures rising vertically instead of receding into space, has been criticized as incoherent. Yet it does have an underlying principle. The picture reads like a multiplication of the half-length devotional images associated with Solario. The brightly colored figures, stacked on top of each other from top to bottom, are equally in focus, and they are all close to the viewer. While not ineffective from a devotional standpoint, this device, spread over the entire picture, produces an effect of claustrophobia. Perhaps in reaction, abbreviated figures have been omitted in the other panels.

Luini's goal of heightening the devotional content of his altarpiece may also be understood in terms of its genesis. His earlier idea for the composition is represented by a pen-and-ink sketch for the main group (fig. 13) in the Louvre.[37] Even for this mature work, the artist did not fail to look back to Foppa's *Lamentation* then in the Milanese church of San Pietro Gessate.[38] There, as in the drawing, Christ's head is lowered over his pendant arm, and both works feature a female figure with arms outflung in desperation.[39] But Luini's main source was an altarpiece of the same theme by Solario (fig. 14), now in the National Gallery of Art, Washington, DC.[40] As with Foppa, Luini's interest in Solario's *Lamentation* is evidenced by his borrowing of specific motifs, in this case, the holy woman bending over to inspect the wounds in Christ's feet, and the grief-stricken John supporting his torso and looking out at the viewer. Luini may even have known some of Solario's preparatory drawings for the altarpiece: the noble type of Christ in San Giorgio resembles a study for the Savior's head by his colleague in the Louvre.[41] Besides Luini's figural repertoire, the colorful effect of the red, orange, and green draperies spread over the altarpiece

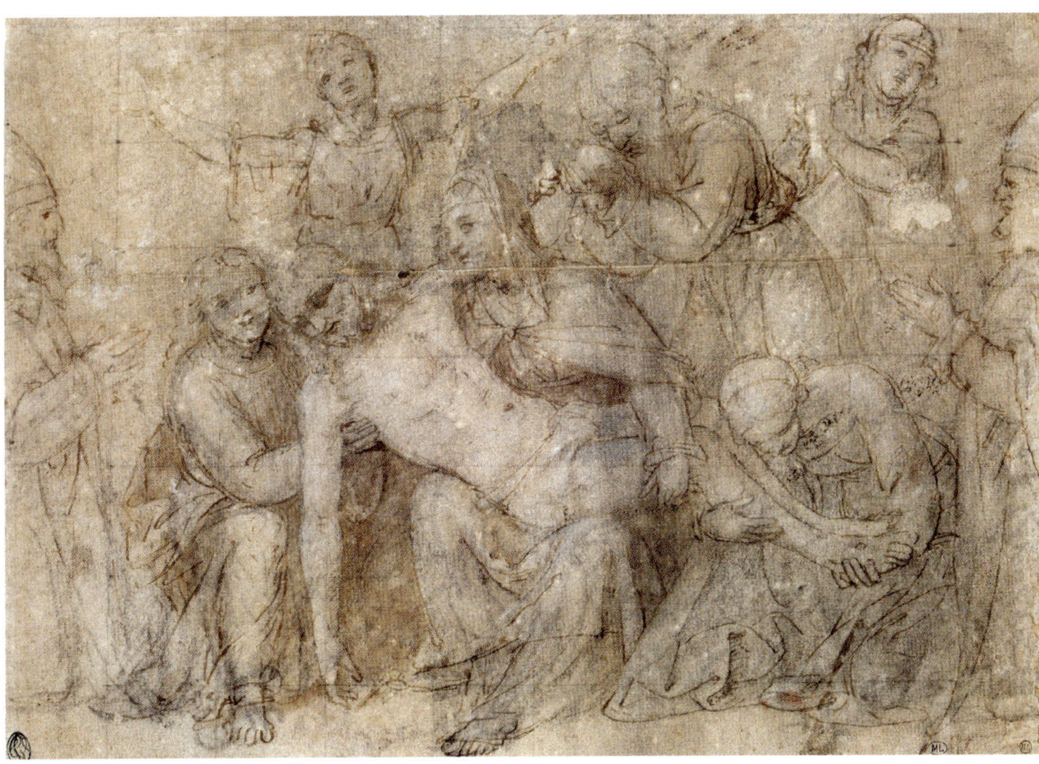

Fig. 13. Bernardino Luini, *Lamentation*, Département des Arts Graphiques, Musée du Louvre, Paris

is also derived from Solario. The high-keyed palette sets the tone for both paintings. But whereas the grief expressed by Solario's figures is uniformly strident, Luini's emotional register is more varied and restrained. The San Giorgio *Lamentation* also avoids Solario's meticulous rendering of detail, as his carefully described textures and surfaces were unnecessary to Luini's purpose of directly communicating a devotional message. Of course, the major difference between the two works lies in their overall composition. Solario's characters, limited in number and clearly separated, are arrayed on a rocky platform before a panoramic landscape. Luini's multi-figured composition eschews this kind of broad expanse. Crowded around the tightly knit central group, a host of half-length figures come into view in a compositional strategy that can only be called experimental. Significantly, Luini never repeated it. But he did return to the protagonists in the picture again and again. A notable example is the adaptive re-use of Christ's arms for the recumbent figure of the naked patriarch in his *Drunkenness of Noah* in the Brera.[42]

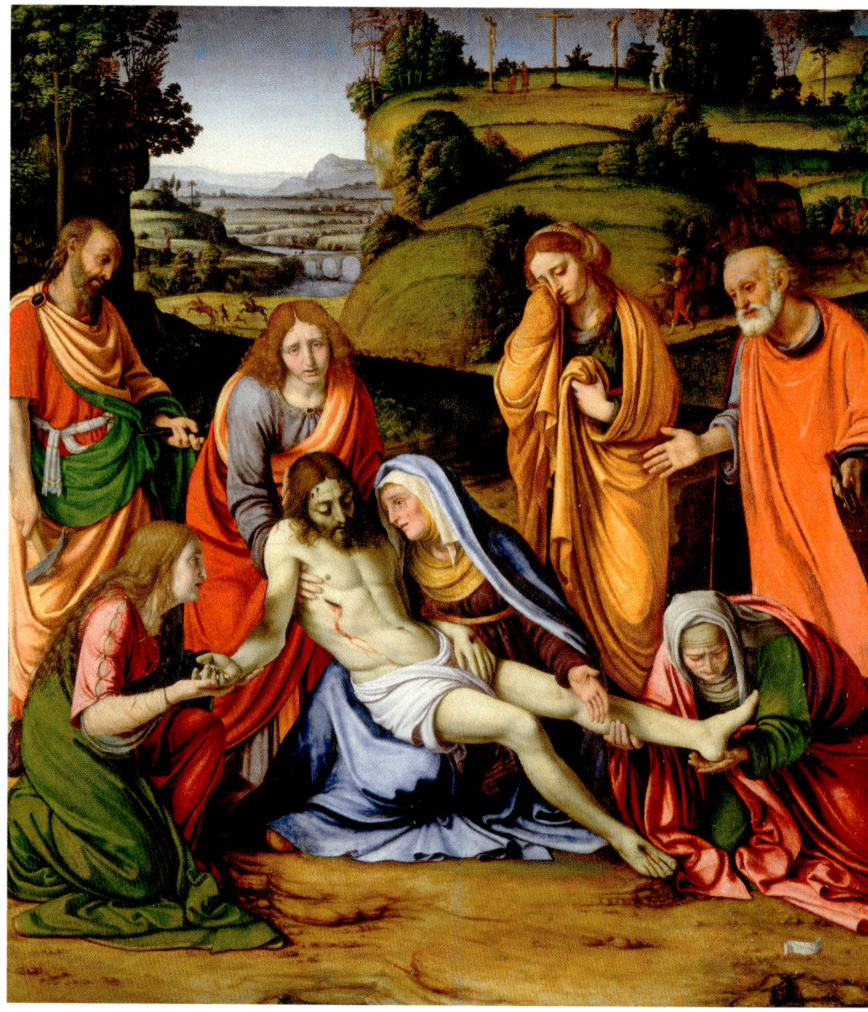

Fig. 14. Andrea Solario, *Lamentation*, Samuel H. Kress Collection, National Gallery of Art, Washington, DC

The densely populated San Giorgio *Lamentation* called out to be simplified in the interest of narrative clarity. Luini's altarpiece (fig. 15), depicting the same subject at a smaller scale, in the Kress Collection at the Museum of Fine Arts, Houston, admirably succeeds in that goal.[43] Scholars have debated whether this work precedes or follows the other *Lamentation*, but the greater unity and legibility of the Houston panel imply a slightly later date.[44] The picture has a vertical rather than a square format, with all but one of the bystanders at San Giorgio eliminated. As in that work, the figures are brought up close to the picture plane and brightly lit against a dark background. Christ sits on a rock in the center of the composition; standing beside him are the Virgin and Saint John, who hold his body upright for contemplation by the viewer. Seated in the lower right, Mary Magdalene supports the Savior's feet on her lap, while a third mourning woman balances John in the upper right corner. Her figure neatly combines the head and hands of two females at San Giorgio. The graceful motif of the Virgin holding her son's lifeless hand was also taken over from the larger *Lamentation*; it stands out amidst the other stiff-limbed gestures meant to lend the figures a kind of authenticity. To this simple and direct arrangement, Luini has added an angelic putto holding the nails of the Crucifixion. Gazing intently at these so-called instruments of the Passion (another is the crown of thorns lying on the shroud), the winged putto may well be Luini's own invention, as he was fond of such creatures. Carolyn Wilson has connected this motif with the relic of the Holy Nail in the Duomo of Milan.[45] The original location of the picture

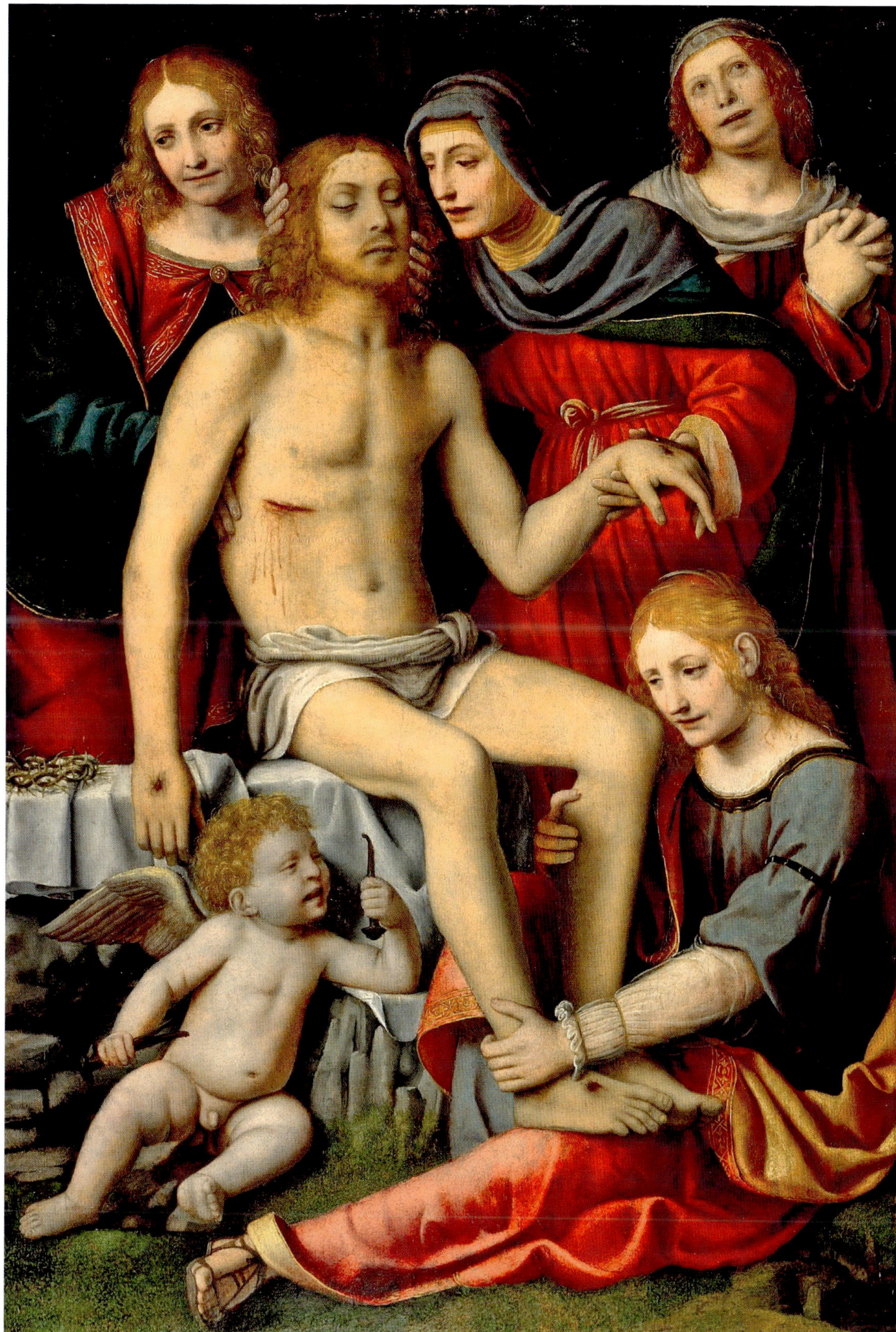

Fig. 15. Bernardino Luini, *Lamentation*, Museum of Fine Arts, Houston

is unknown, but, given its subject, it may have been completed, like the larger altarpiece in San Giorgio, for the chapel of a confraternity dedicated to the Corpus Christi.

If the Houston *Lamentation* follows the San Giorgio altarpiece, the third in a sequence of progressively reduced treatments of the theme is a hitherto unknown *Pietà* (fig. 16), here published for the first time. The attribution of this recently discovered work to Luini is attested by its resemblance in style and iconography to the documented *Lamentation* in the chapel of the Holy Sacrament. Composed of a single wood plank measuring 40.3 by 49.6 cm, the panel retains its original dimensions except for the bottom edge, where saw marks and a few small losses suggest that it was reduced at some time in the past. Restoration in 2005 removed a coat of yellowed varnish that obscured the underlying paint layers, which proved to be in good condition. The figures, shown half-length, are arranged in a horizontal format. As in the two previous *Lamentations*, they are brought up close to the picture plane and boldly illuminated against a dark background, and they, too, lack haloes. The Virgin, wearing a dark blue and green robe and a light blue head-covering over a transparent veil, holds her son upright, while the youthful Saint John, in a contrasting red tunic, looks on at right. The two figures have exchanged the places they held in the preceding compositions. The Savior's head is tilted to the left and lowered, as in the preparatory sketch (fig. 13) for the San Giorgio picture, and his arms fall at his sides. He wears no crown of thorns.

Stripped of a supporting cast and with no extraneous details, the *Pietà* distills the Lamentation theme to its essence. In extreme close-up, Christ's companions thrust his lifeless body toward the viewer, whose opportunity to scrutinize their faces heightens the emotional response. Unlike the anguished mourners in the previous *Lamentations*, the Virgin and Saint John here exhibit a tender compassion or concern. With its muted expression of grief, the image acts on the pious spectator more as a solace than as a prompt to share Christ's suffering. Interaction with the beholder was clearly of great importance to Luini, and while the patron for whom he painted the picture remains unknown, it was presumably intended for private worship and meditation in a house or monastic cell.

As a recipient of the donor's prayers, the *Pietà* was more than an excerpt from the *Lamentation*. Formally simple yet rich with thematic meaning, the spiritual triad of the Virgin, Christ, and Saint John would also have evoked the *Crucifixion*, where Mary and John stand on either side of the cross. And, with its upright figure of the dead Christ, Luini's composition further alludes to the traditional *Imago Pietatis* (Man of Sorrows). The complex iconography underlying the picture extends to the motif of the Virgin embracing Christ, which recalls the Byzantine type of *eleousa*, where she holds the Child in a similar manner. Like Mary, John joined the icon of the Man of Sorrows at an early date, and there are numerous representations of the three-figure group in Lombard devotional painting, including the pinnacle of Bergognone's *Saint Jerome* altarpiece of ca. 1495–1500 in the Brera.[16] Luini's picture, nevertheless, eschews the tears, wounds, and blood droplets that typify these depictions, in favor of a tenderly intimate portrayal, in which the Virgin rests her head on Christ's shoulder and John gently touches the Savior's arm. The formula of the outward-facing Christ, flanked by mourners, is given great immediacy, then, by the way John's figure is sharply cropped, as if he had just come upon the scene. His emotive profile recalls that of the ardent Phillip to the right of Christ in Leonardo's *Last Supper*.

Confirmation that the *Pietà* closes the series of Passion pictures comes from its stylistic resemblance to the altarpiece that Luini

Fig. 16. Bernardino Luini, *Pietà*, Private collection

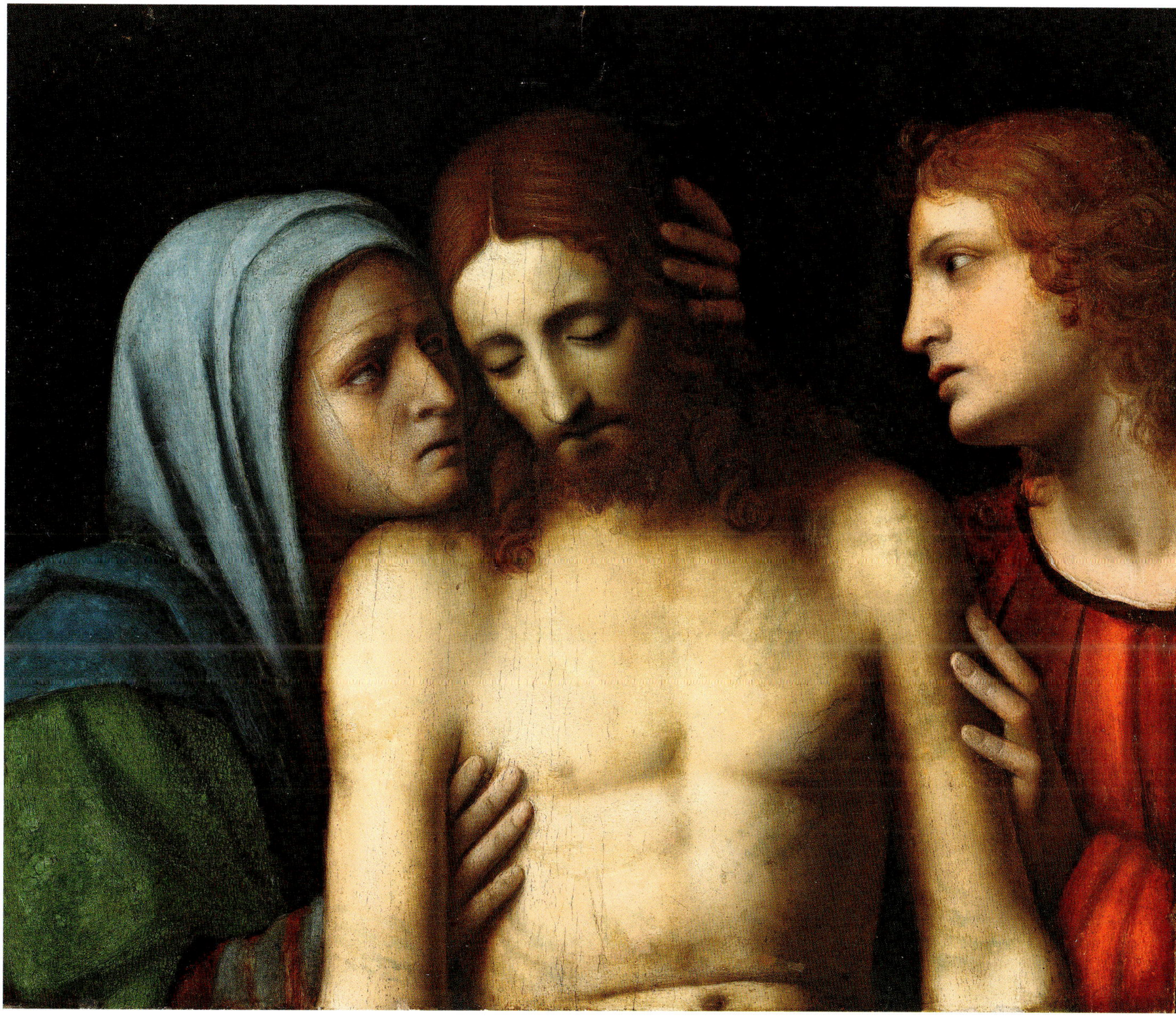

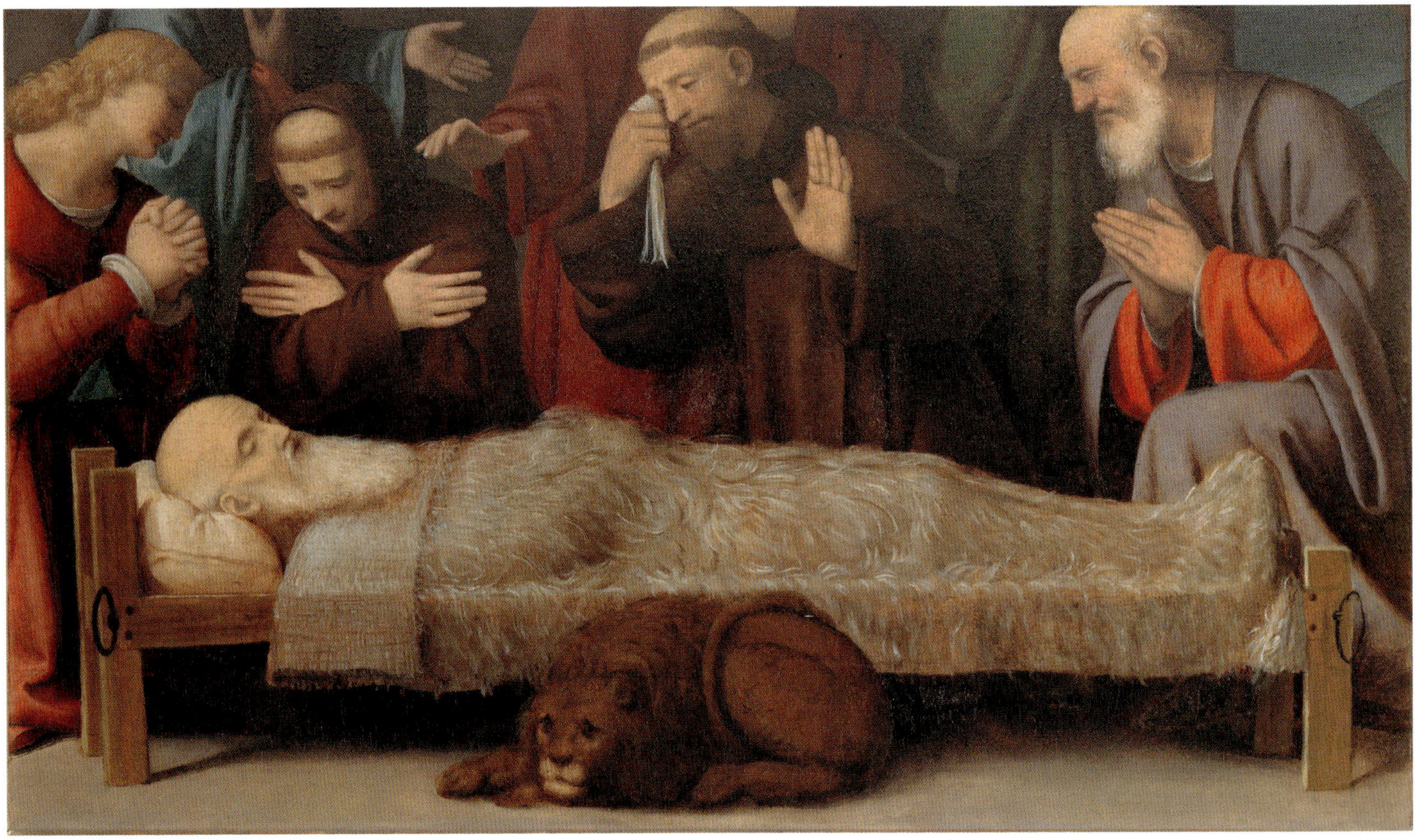

painted for the chapel of Saint Jerome in Como Cathedral. That polyptych features the saint among others surrounding the Virgin and in the predella below the main compartment. In addition to being signed, this is one of Luini's few securely datable works, owing to the presence of the donor Scaramuccia Trivulzio, who was briefly a cardinal in 1517/18.[47] The oblong predella panel (fig. 17), depicting the death of Saint Jerome, borrows the figure of a mourner with clasped hands from the San Giorgio *Lamentation* and, with its darkened setting and subtly illuminated figures, is especially close in style to the *Pietà*. Again Leonardo is a reference point: the head of the music-making angel seated below the Virgin's throne is a direct quotation from the *Virgin of the Rocks*. The formal and expressive qualities that link the *Pietà* and the Trivulzio altarpiece reappear in Luini's *Crucifixion* (fig. 18) in the State Hermitage Museum, St. Petersburg.[48] But here the discreet shadows of the *Sacra Conversazione* have given way to a deeper chiaroscuro more consonant with the subject. The *Crucifixion* is datable stylistically between the Trivulzio altarpiece and another *Sacra Conversazione* in the Brera, of 1521, providing a collocation for the *Pietà* late in the second decade of the artist's career. The physiognomies and hand gestures of the figures in the Hermitage panel are almost interchangeable with those in the *Pietà*, as is the somber mood in both pictures.

Not long after completing the *Pietà*, an event occurred that marked a turning point in Luini's career. Around the time of Leonardo's death in France on May 2, 1519, his two closest disciples, Gian Giacomo Caprotti called Salai and Francesco Melzi, brought back to Milan a treasure trove of works by and after the master. Salai (meaning "devil") entered Leonardo's employ at the age of ten, in 1490.

Fig. 17. Bernardino Luini, *Death of Saint Jerome*, predella panel from the St. Jerome Altarpiece, Cathedral, Como

Fig. 18. Bernardino Luini, *Crucifixion*, State Hermitage Museum, St. Petersburg

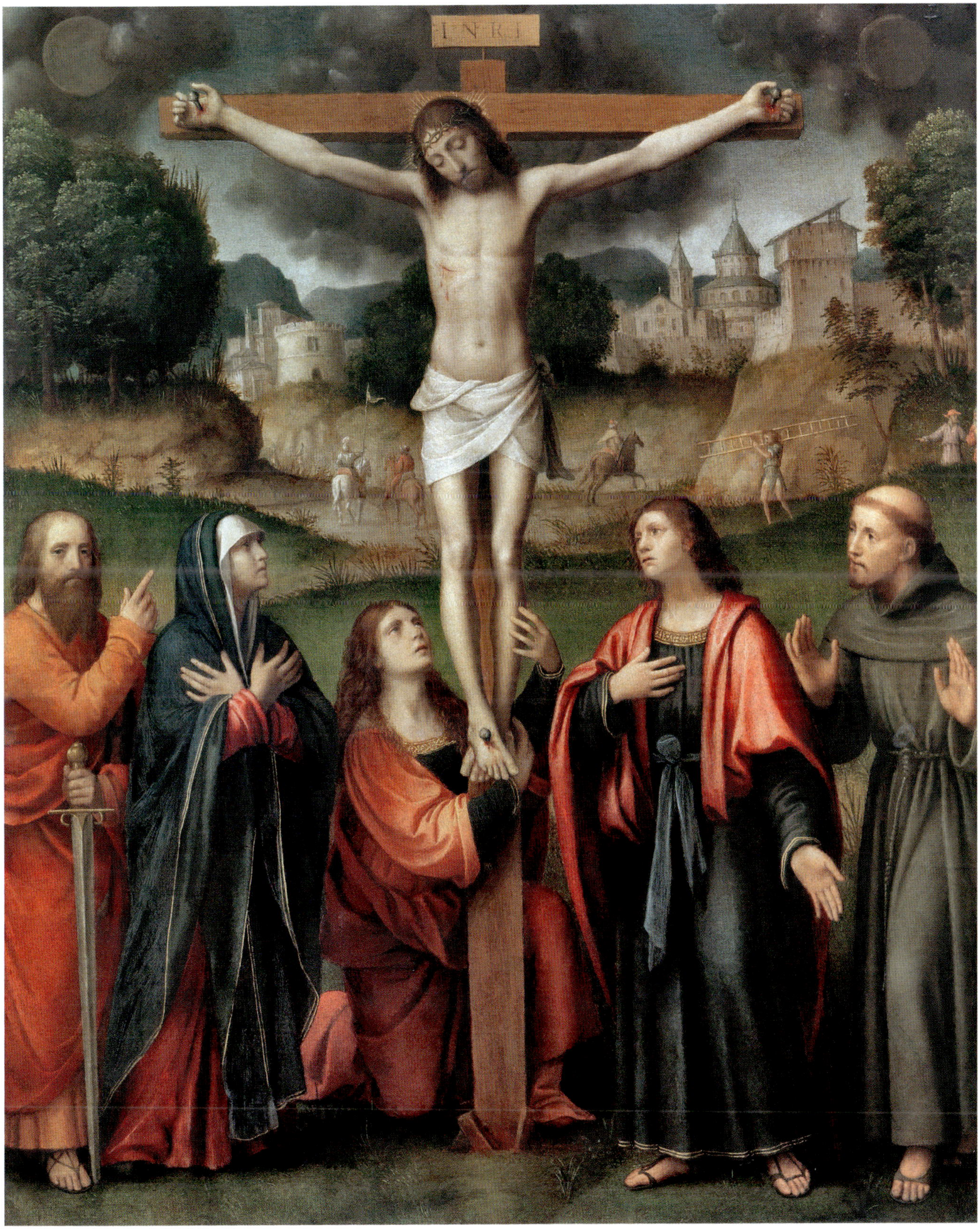

Despite his misconduct (Leonardo calls him a liar, glutton, and thief), the youth, graced with curly hair, became the artist's lifelong companion. The reason for their attachment, Vasari makes clear, was the strong attraction Leonardo felt for Salai's physical beauty. In his will the painter left his pupil some property in Milan but no paintings or other works of art. This has been taken to mean that Salai was merely a servant or shop assistant. But his pictorial ability became evident when, in 2007, a version (fig. 19) of Leonardo's recently reidentified *Salvator Mundi*, signed by Salai and dated 1511, turned up on the art market.[49] This work is now in the Pinacoteca Ambrosiana, Milan. Not surprisingly, perhaps, the scoundrel was shot dead in 1524. The inventory of his possessions, compiled the following year, lists several paintings associated with Leonardo, including a *Mona Lisa*, a *Saint John the Baptist*, a *Leda*, and a *Saint Anne*. The high valuations placed on these works was taken to support the idea that they were Leonardo's originals repatriated by Salai.[50] But another recently discovered document states that, in 1518 – while Leonardo was still alive – Salai, in Milan, was paid a very large sum by King Francis I for a group of paintings likely to be the autograph works with the same titles that are today in the Louvre.[51] The pictures cited in the inventory were evidently by Salai. In the absence of the originals, these and other "official" copies made in the studio by his closest pupils served as records of the master's work.

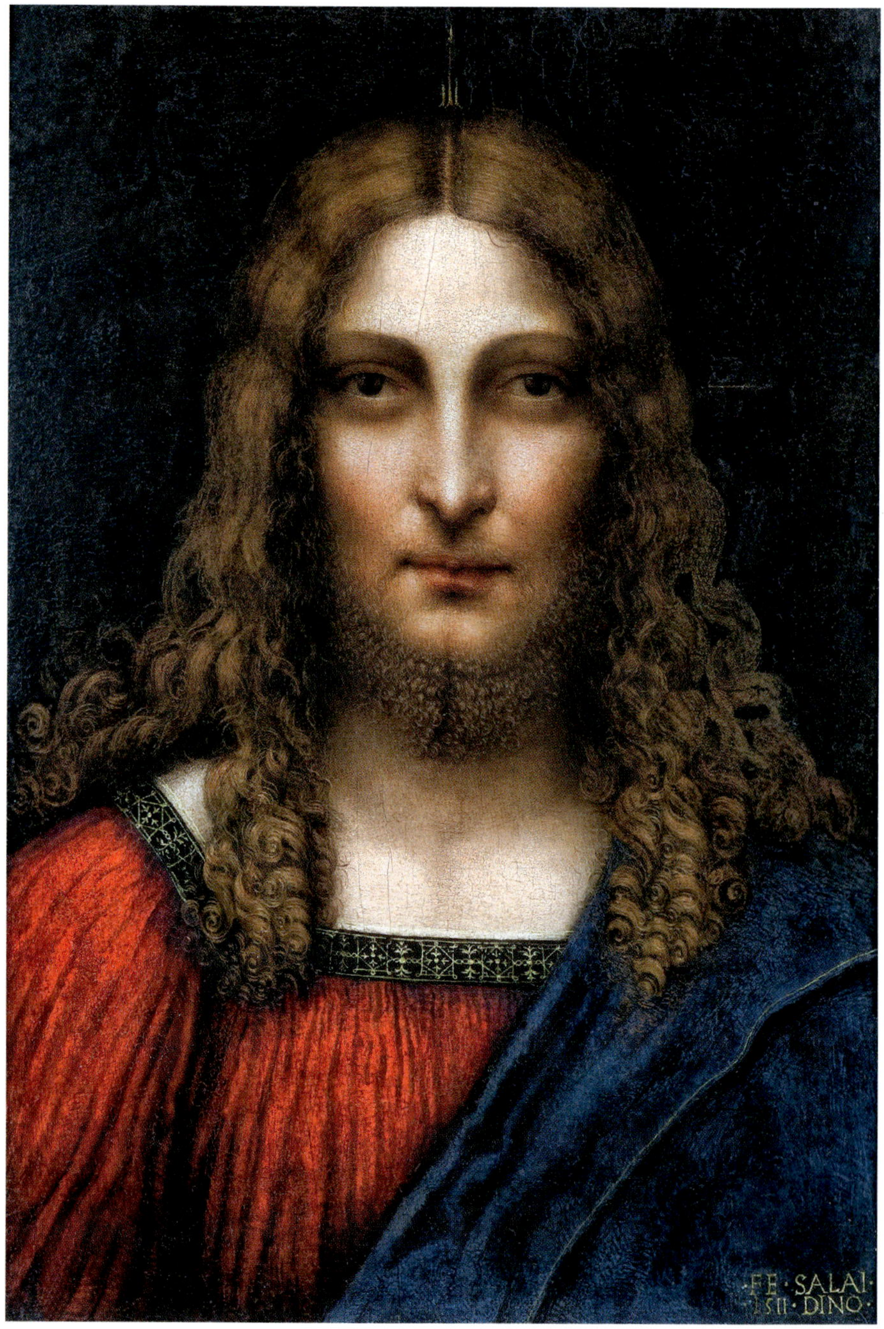

Fig. 19. Gian Giacomo Caprotti called Salai, *Bust of Christ*, Veneranda Biblioteca Ambrosiana, Milan

Leonardo's favorite pupil Francesco Melzi, forty years his junior, was born in 1491/93 and died about 1570. After Leonardo returned to Milan in 1508, Melzi's family commissioned him to remodel their villa at Vaprio d'Adda north of the city. The project came to nothing, but Leonardo and Francesco developed a deep friendship that lasted the rest of their lives. Handsome, like the incorrigible Salai, but far more cultivated, the young nobleman also accompanied the master on his trips to Rome and France. And in the will that he made shortly before he died, Leonardo bequeathed all his manuscripts, drawings, and materials relating to his art to Melzi.[52] The heir then brought the notebooks, amounting to thousands of pages, and the scarcely less numerous drawings back to Milan and kept them at the villa. There Melzi devoted himself to preserving the master's legacy, organizing the vast corpus of works on paper and eventually compiling Leonardo's notes on painting as the *Trattato della Pittura* (Codex Urbinas Latinus 1270 in the Vatican Library). He also copied some of Leonardo's drawings, including a few that do not survive. In this way, Villa Melzi became a shrine to Leonardo's memory with his former pupil as the keeper of the flame. An agent of the duke of Ferrara visited the villa in 1523, where he was shown "those notebooks of Leonardo, with the anatomical studies and many other fine things."[53] And on his pilgrimage to Vaprio in 1566, Giorgio Vasari also admired the anatomical drawings (now in the Royal Library, Windsor Castle), which the artist had made for a projected treatise.[54] But neither of these visitors mentions the most outstanding artwork Melzi had inherited, the cartoon (fig. 6) of the *Virgin and Child with Saint Anne and John the Baptist*, perhaps because it was no longer in his possession.

Even before becoming its owner, the cartoon played a central role in Melzi's far from prolific activity as a painter. His signed *Youth with a Parrot* is in a Milanese private collection.[55] Completed long after his time with Leonardo, in 1551, this inept portrait of a fashionably dressed sitter shows that Melzi's skill in painting, as in drawing, was that of a copyist or imitator. He had no pictorial imagination of his own. Because it depends on Leonardo, the artist's *Vertumnus and Pomona* (fig. 20) in the Gemäldegalerie, Berlin, is much more successful as a work of art. Proudly signed with his name in (now mostly effaced) Greek letters, this work is impressive partly on account of its scale.[56] The figures are equal in size to those in the cartoon, which Melzi took as a model. The painting depicts the Roman god of the seasons Vertumnus, in the guise of an old woman, attempting to woo the beautiful Pomona. This tale from Ovid's *Metamorphoses* also prompted the motif of the grapevine encircling the tree immediately behind the figures, which symbolizes togetherness. Melzi's Pomona, seated on a rocky ledge, effectively translates the Virgin's figure in the cartoon into painted form. The artist retained Mary's facial type and pose but changed her costume to a décolletage and substituted a basket of fruit for the infant Christ. The distant mountains in the picture similarly render Leonardo's sketchy landscape in shades of blue and gray. The face of Vertumnus, gently touching Pomona's shoulder, recalls, in reverse, another drawing, the *Profile of an Old Man*, signed twice by Melzi and dated 1510, in the Biblioteca Ambrosiana, Milan.[57] The disguised man's profile, facing right in the drawing, is a characteristic type reflecting Leonardo's interest in facial structure.

But when did Melzi paint the *Vertumnus and Pomona*? An approximate date for the picture is provided by a double-sided sheet from the so-called Codex Resta also in the Ambrosiana. On the recto of the sheet is Melzi's red chalk study for Pomona's right foot together with a mountain range sketched in by Leonardo.[58] Melzi's preparatory study, and by implication the painting for which it was made, thus dates to Leonardo's lifetime. A more precise date during the master's Roman sojourn in 1513–16 is suggested by the context for the painting as an example of the new artistic genre of erotic mythologies pioneered by Raphael and others in the Eternal City. Leonardo's own exercise in the genre was the *Leda and the Swan*, which, together with the London cartoon, seems to have inspired Melzi, just as it did Raphael. Having initiated the project in Florence, Leonardo continued to work on the painting, which may have been among those sold by Salai to the French king. Known today only in copies, the picture (fig. 21) represented the nude Leda standing next to her suitor, the god Jupiter disguised as a swan. Leda's expression resembles Pomona's, smiling and glancing modestly downwards, as does her elaborately

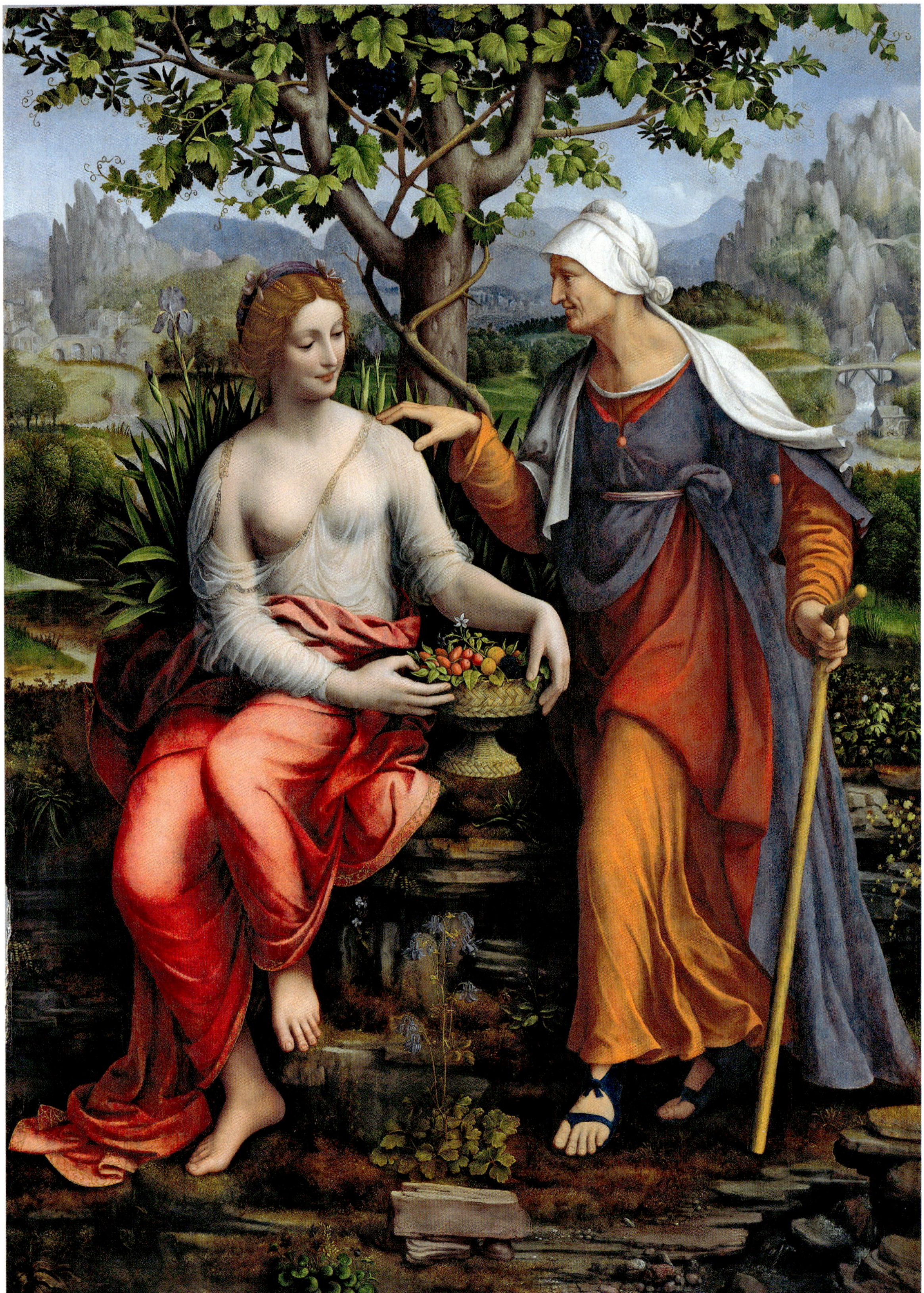

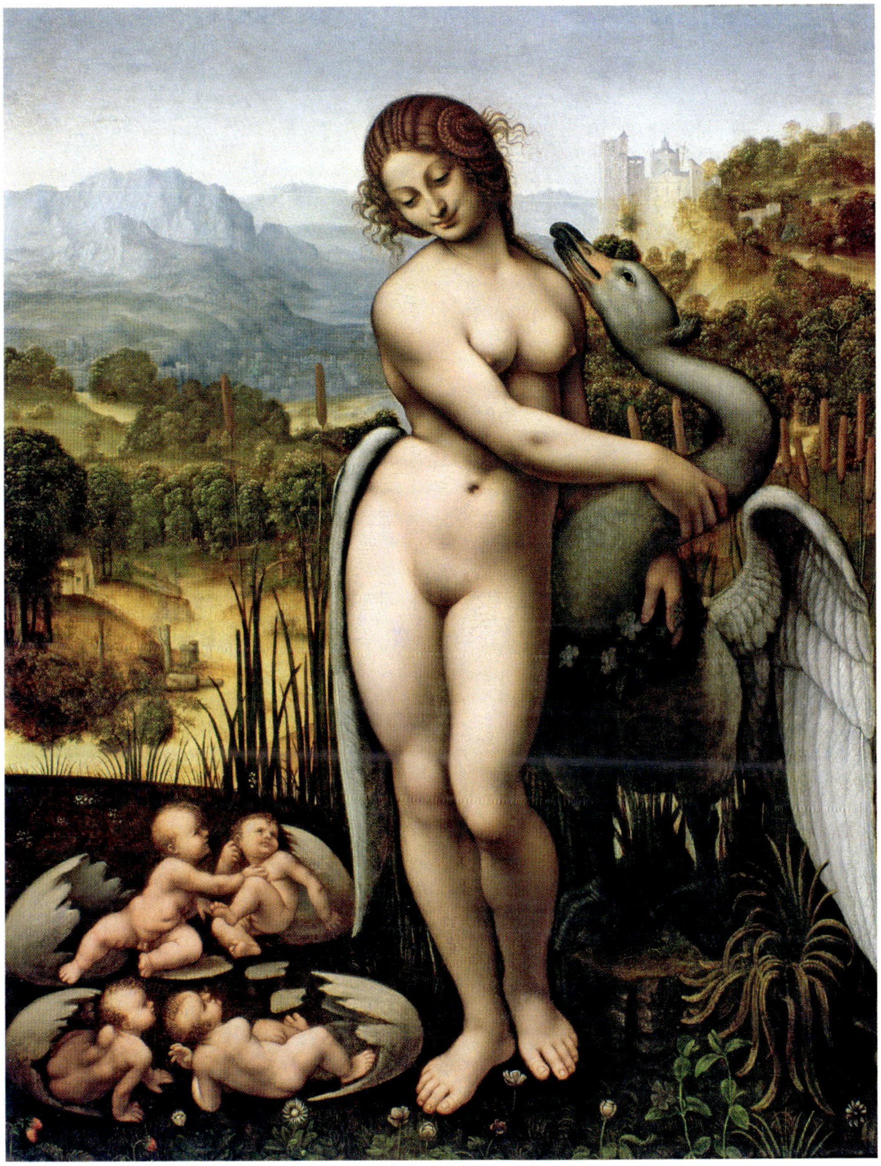

Fig. 20. Francesco Melzi, *Vertumnus and Pomona*, Gemäldegalerie, Staatliche Museen, Berlin

Fig. 21. Cesare da Sesto, after Leonardo da Vinci, *Leda and the Swan*, Earl of Pembroke Collection, Wilton House, Salisbury

Following pages

Fig. 22. Francesco Melzi, *Flora*, State Hermitage Museum, St. Petersburg

Fig. 23. Bernardino Luini, *Flora*, Galleria Borghese, Rome

braided headdress (actually a wig). Scattered around the foreground in the *Leda* was a profusion of flowering plants similar to the carefully observed iris behind Pomona, and the columbine at her feet, likewise symbolizing romantic love. Melzi probably completed the *Vertumnus and Pomona* under Leonardo's supervision: the revealing transparency of her garment and the fluttering folds of his dress, suggesting that the god has just arrived, like the infant Baptist in the cartoon, may well reflect his thinking.

As a mythology, the *Vertumnus and Pomona* is not unique in Melzi's oeuvre. A smaller panel (transferred to canvas) of *Flora* (fig. 22), in the Hermitage, having been accredited to Leonardo, is now universally accepted as his pupil's work.[59] The sensuality of Melzi's depiction is heightened by the fact that Flora appears as a single figure without the wind-god Zephyrus, who, according to legend, transformed the nymph Chloris into the goddess of flowers (the event shown in Botticelli's *Primavera*). Seated in a rocky grotto surrounded by plants and flowers, Flora is a variant of Pomona. She sports the same coiffure and reflects the same models, namely, Leda and the Virgin in the London cartoon, but at three-quarter length and without the contrapposto. The goddess wears a ruby brooch and a white dress, with stylized gold flowers, loosened to expose one breast. Restoration of the picture in 2016–18 revealed that her brilliant blue robe is pure ultramarine, a costly pigment the well-to-do artist could afford.

As with *Vertumnus and Pomona*, Leonardo might be called the intellectual author behind the painting. In both works, as in the *Leda*, a recurring theme is the abundance of nature. The landscape owes much to Leonardo, not only the grotto, which recalls that of the *Virgin of the Rocks*, but also the meticulously rendered plants and flowers. Framed by ivy, on the right, and fern, on the left, the goddess grasps a spray of jasmine, instead of a basket of fruit, while holding up a sprig of columbine, which she contemplates, like the Christ Child scrutinizing a bloom in Leonardo's early Benois *Madonna* also in the Hermitage. The source for this aspect of the picture is, again, the *Leda*, whose female protagonist similarly holds flowers she has just picked. Taken individually, the plants in the Hermitage picture, like the grapevine, iris, and columbine in *Vertumnus and Pomona*, display the kind of accuracy found in the botanical studies Leonardo used primarily for the *Leda*.[60] The plants

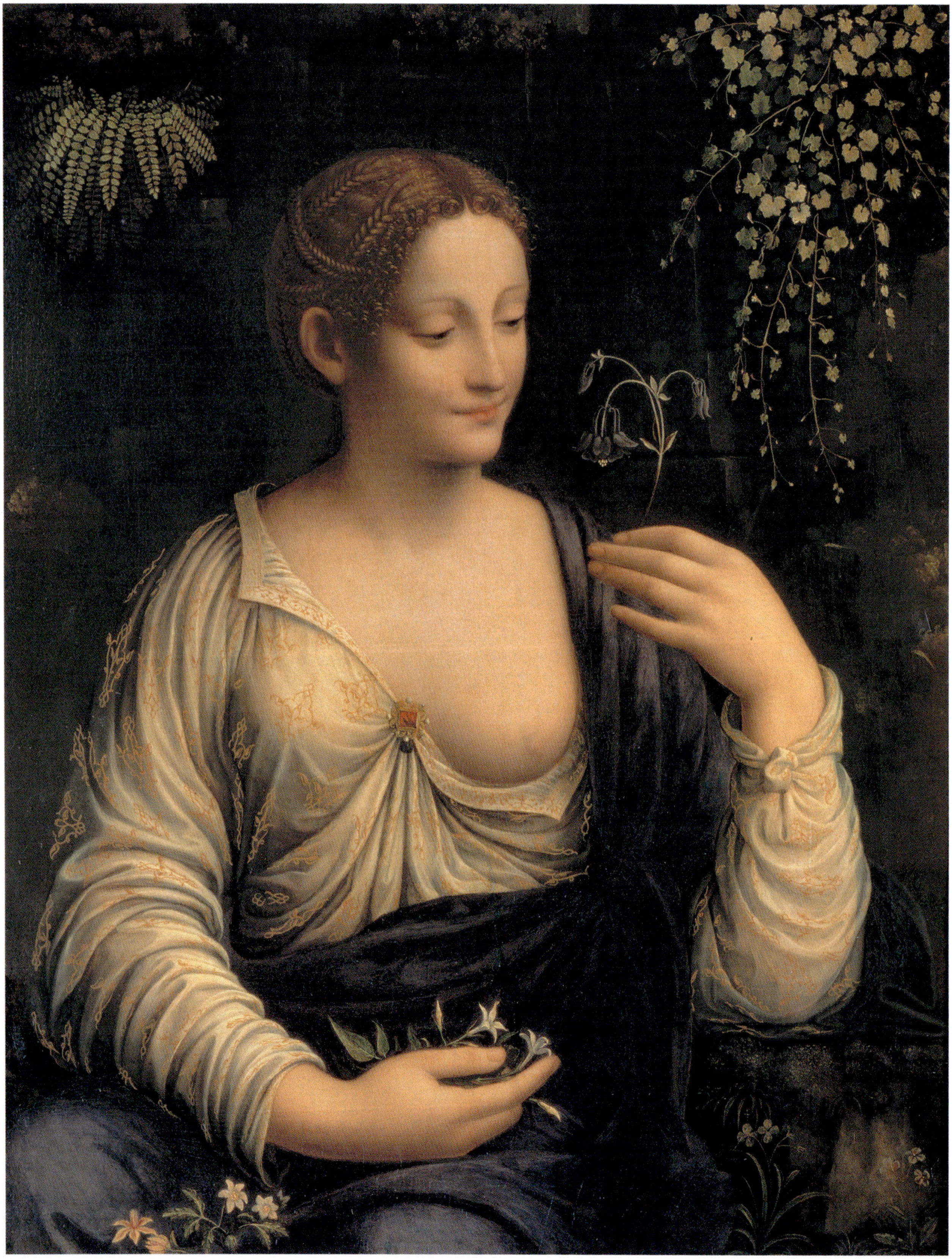

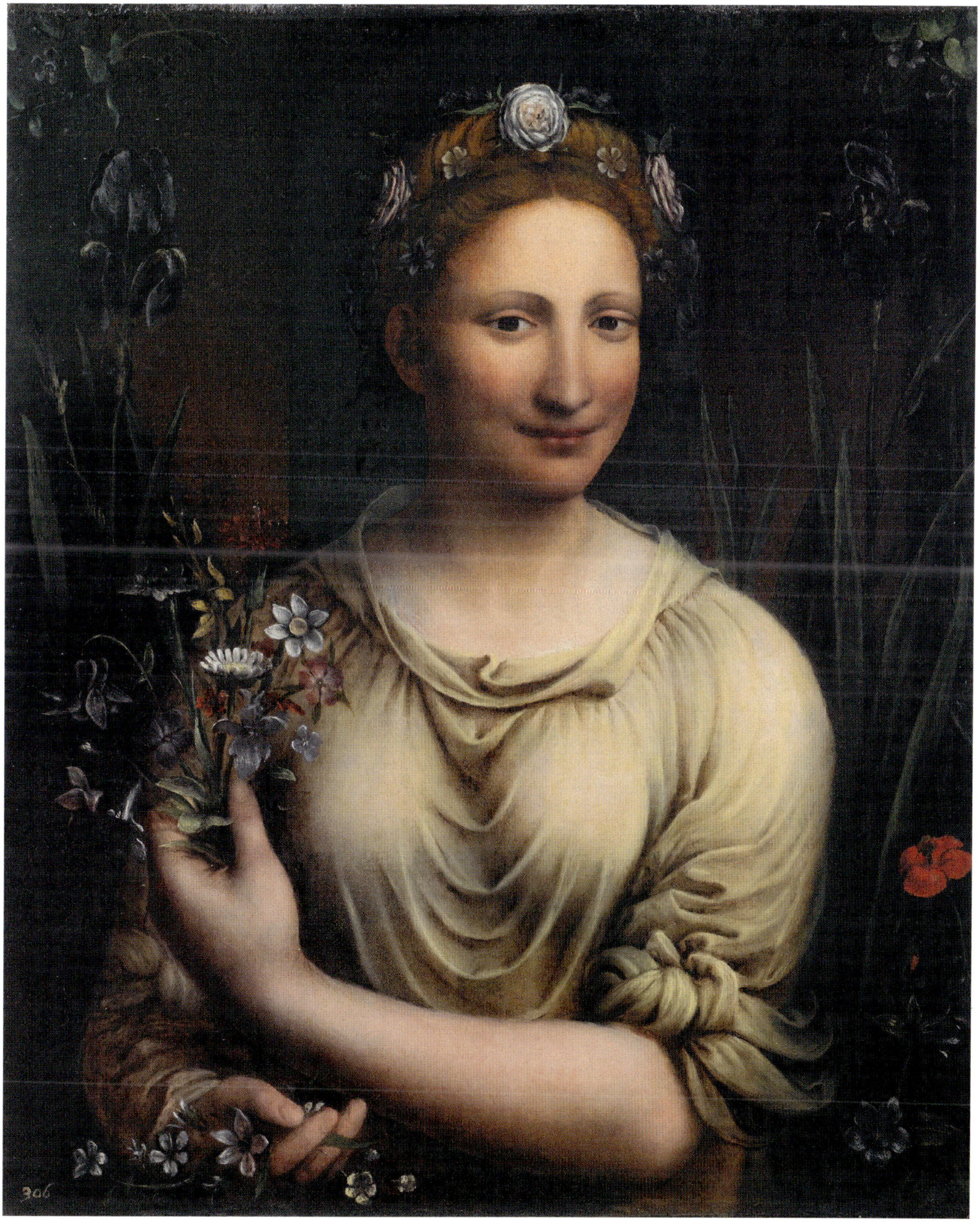

in Melzi's pictures, symbolizing romantic love, have the character of carefully observed specimens pointing to their origin in the master's drawings. They do not match any of Leonardo's extant studies, but Melzi is known to have copied such works, which, in the case of his mythologies, do not survive.[61]

Leonardo's heir returned to Milan sometime between August 1519, when he was still in France, and March 1523, when a document places him in his native city.[62] In addition to Leonardo's graphic legacy, Melzi may also have brought back *Flora*, unless Francis I, who paid him a salary, acquired the picture, first recorded in the French royal collection in 1649. But whether in France or Italy, Melzi's painting seems to have enjoyed considerable renown, as attested by several copies.[63] These suggest that the *Flora* was admired not only for its pagan allure but also because of its association with Leonardo. A similar painting (fig. 23) of the same subject is in the Galleria Borghese, Rome. This variant of the *Flora* was apparently based on Melzi's picture or on a full-scale cartoon for it that is no longer extant. The Borghese *Flora* is generally taken to be Melzi's on account of its resemblance to his version of the theme, but it is manifestly by Bernardino Luini. Though recently said to come from his studio, the work has the look, after a recent cleaning, of a fully autograph production by Luini dating to the early 1520s.[64] A related drawing by him of Pomona's fruit-crowned head, in the British Museum, hints that he may have considered the two females as a pair, rather the way that Melzi seems to have done.[65] But while surrounding her with flowers, Luini recasts Flora in a different light. His half-length figure is not self-absorbed, like Melzi's, but smiles broadly out at the viewer. And, differently from Melzi's elegantly attired yet provocative goddess, Luini's is fully clothed in a plain white chemise with a sleeve rolled up. Far from remote or mysterious, this Flora is an affable, outgoing woman of the people. Crowned with roses, she holds up a variegated floral bouquet. Like the irises framing her head, these blossoms are readily identifiable, but they lack the botanical accuracy of the plants in Melzi's *Flora* or *Vertumnus and Pomona*. Unlike Leonardo's disciple, Luini did not have access to – or failed to take an interest in – the master's carefully observed nature studies that Melzi employed to lend scientific precision to his paintings.

Another category of drawings by and after Leonardo does seem to have caught Luini's attention, however. Three repeated profiles of an old man, facing left, bring together both artists with Melzi acting as an intermediary. This remarkable sequence suggests that, not long after Melzi's return, Luini encountered this and other works by Leonardo, which he would not otherwise have known, at Vaprio d'Adda. The first in the series was the master's own red chalk study (fig. 24) in the Hamburger Kunsthalle.[66] Though now less popular than in past centuries, Leonardo's caricatures or, more accurately, grotesque heads, concerned as they are with human physiognomy, are central to his achievement.[67] The Hamburg sheet portrays the subject with a low forehead, pug nose, and jutting chin. The same deformities recur, then, in Melzi's copy (fig. 25), also in red chalk and at the same diminutive scale, in the Royal Collection at Windsor Castle.[68] The pupil's attempt to accurately reproduce the original even led him to imitate Leonardo's left-handed shading. The third profile in the series (fig. 26) has been detached from a sheet in the Ambrosiana, with other studies by Luini, the reverse of which is inscribed with his name "louino."[69] The medium is the same, but Luini makes no effort to reproduce the original exactly. Closer to Melzi, his version appears to be a copy of a copy.

Luini not only imitated one of Leonardo's grotesque physiognomies; he may also have owned a number of them. According to

Fig. 24. Leonardo da Vinci, *Head of an Old Man in Profile*, Kunsthalle, Hamburg

Fig. 25. Francesco Melzi after Leonardo da Vinci, *Head of an Old Man in Profile*, Royal Collection, Windsor Castle

Fig. 26. Bernardino Luini after Francesco Melzi or Leonardo da Vinci, *Head of an Old Man in Profile*, Veneranda Biblioteca Ambrosiana, Milan

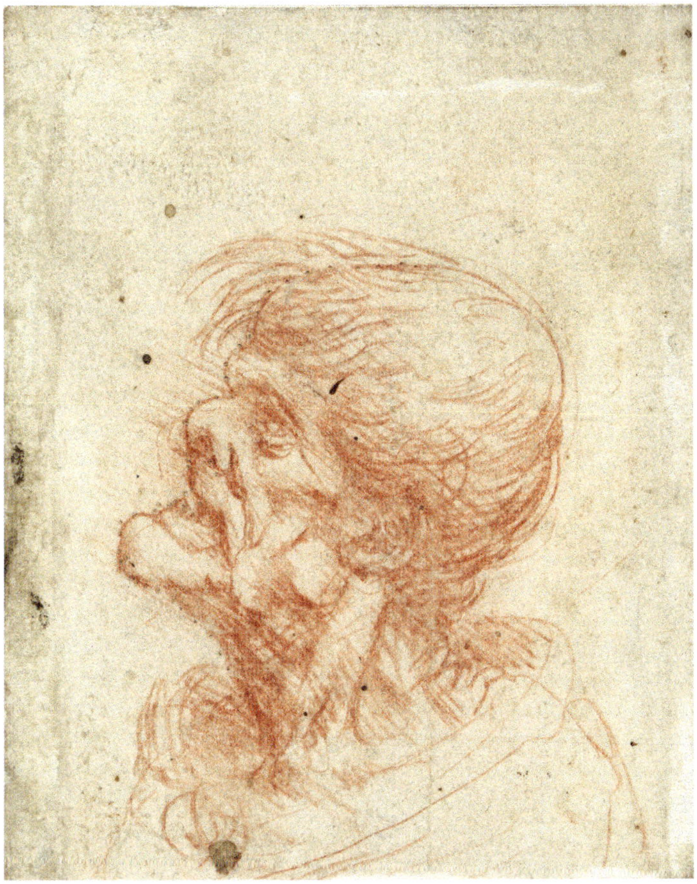

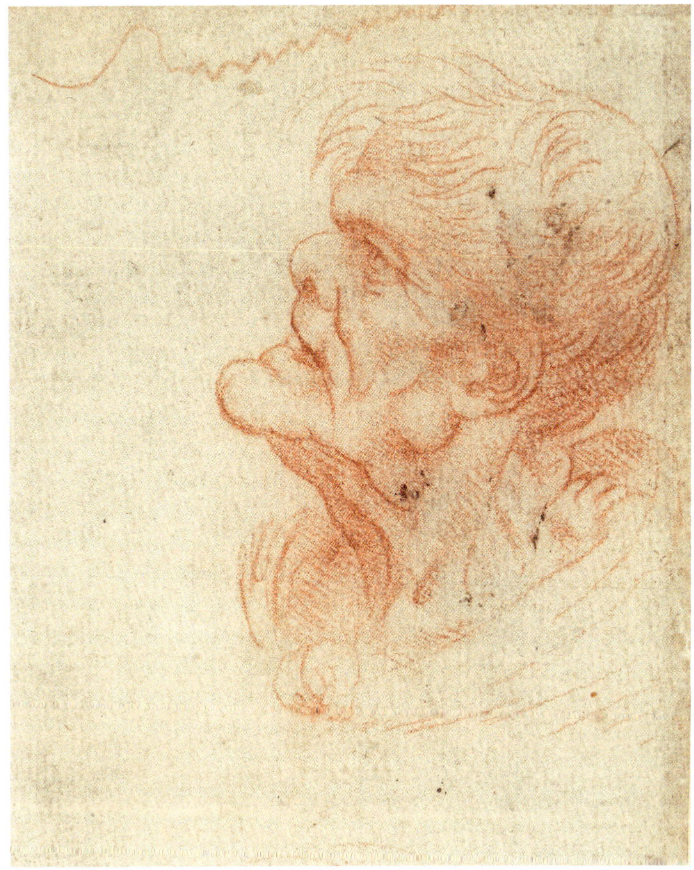

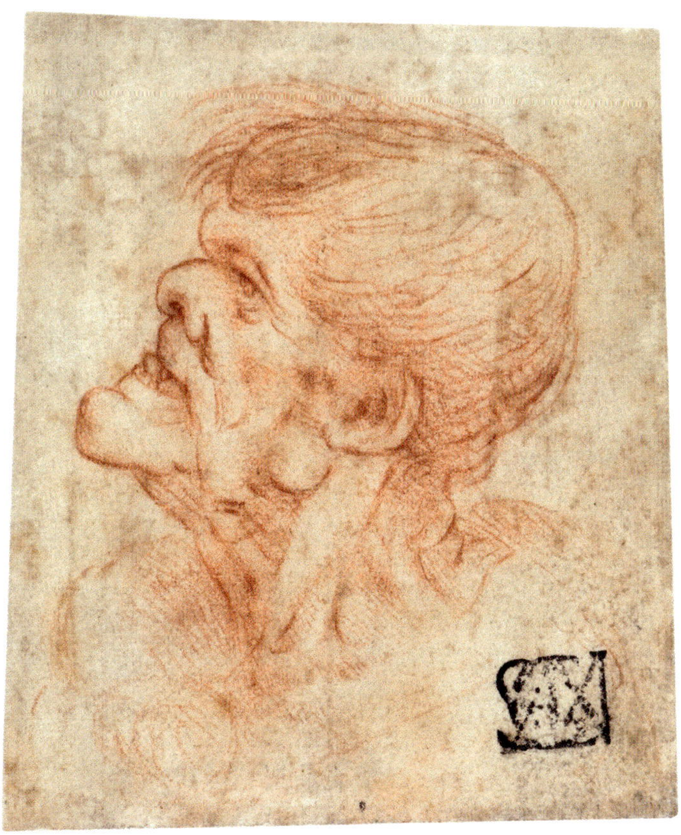

Lomazzo, a *libricciuolo* (little book) of fifty of these drawings by the master, depicting the heads of old people and peasants, belonged to Luini's youngest son Aurelio.[70] Born only two years before Bernardino died, Aurelio, also a painter, broke with his father's tradition and embarked on a new style influenced by Central Italian art. He remained interested in Leonardo, however, and Carmen Bambach has convincingly attributed to him a sheet with five physiognomic studies in the British Museum, ostensibly inspired by the album he owned.[71] Quite possibly, the book of "visi mostruosi," or monstrous faces, as Lomazzo calls them, may already have belonged to Bernardino, from whom it passed by descent to his son.

The most notable of Leonardo's physiognomies was the so-called "nutcracker" profile of an old man with a hooked nose, protruding lower lip, and prominent chin. This type was repeated over and over again by the master and his circle.[72] Leonardo's fascination with bizarre characters was shared by Luini, who used them for the figures of evildoers in his works. A prime example is his *Christ among the Doctors* (fig. 27) in the National Gallery, London.[73] Once famous as a Leonardo masterpiece, this panel painting includes, at right, the profile of a doctor, or theologian, disputing with Christ, which exhibits the characteristic aquiline type. His figure, together with those of the other disputants, is contrasted with the centrally placed Christ, who recalls another Leonardo model, namely, the *Salvator Mundi* copied by Salai (fig. 19). Isabella d'Este, already mentioned as a patron of Leonardo's, asked him to paint a picture of Christ at the age when he disputed with the doctors, but this work was never executed and is known today only in the form of echoes of the composition by the young Correggio and others. The design of a single Christ may have reached the stage of a cartoon, however, to which Luini, if he knew it, typically added the doctors in order to clarify the subject. Posed frontally, Christ addresses the viewer as if he or she also had to be convinced. Though a mere boy in the scriptural account, Luini's Christ is approximated to the adult Savior, only younger. The inclusion of the doctors in the picture argues that by this time (the late 1520s), the artist grasped the principle of contrasting types of youth and age, beauty and ugliness, and virtue and vice that underlies so much of Leonardo's work.

As part of Leonardo's graphic legacy, Melzi also seems to have brought the *Virgin and Child with Saint Anne and the Infant Saint John the Baptist* (fig. 6) back to Milan. And it was there, presumably ensconced in Melzi's villa, that Luini apparently gained access to the cartoon, an encounter that would radically transform his style. Previously, his experience of Leonardo was limited; now he was able to study, in depth, one of the master's greatest achievements. The evidence for this engagement is Luini's copy, quoting the figure composition, in his own painting of the *Holy Family with Saint Anne and the Infant John the Baptist* (fig. 28) in the Ambrosiana.[74] Again according to Lomazzo, the cartoon belonged in his time to Luini's son Aurelio.[75] His ownership of this drawing, in addition to the album of caricatures, has suggested to scholars that it may have belonged earlier to Bernardino, from whom it descended to Aurelio.[76] In this scenario, Melzi would have given the cartoon to the elder Luini either before or after the latter painted his copy. In any case, the Ambrosiana painting's dependence on the cartoon is undeniable.

The first to note and evaluate this debt was Cardinal Federico Borromeo (1564–1641), archbishop of Milan and founder of the venerable institution that houses Luini's picture. A great collector and patron of the arts, Borromeo established the Ambrosiana, consisting of a library, an art academy, and a museum.[77] His holdings of works by different Italian masters, displayed in the Pinacoteca

Fig. 27. Bernardino Luini, *Christ among the Doctors*, The National Gallery, London

Following pages
Figs. 28a-b. Bernardino Luini, *Holy Family with Saint Anne and the Infant John the Baptist*, whole and detail, Veneranda Biblioteca Ambrosiana, Milan

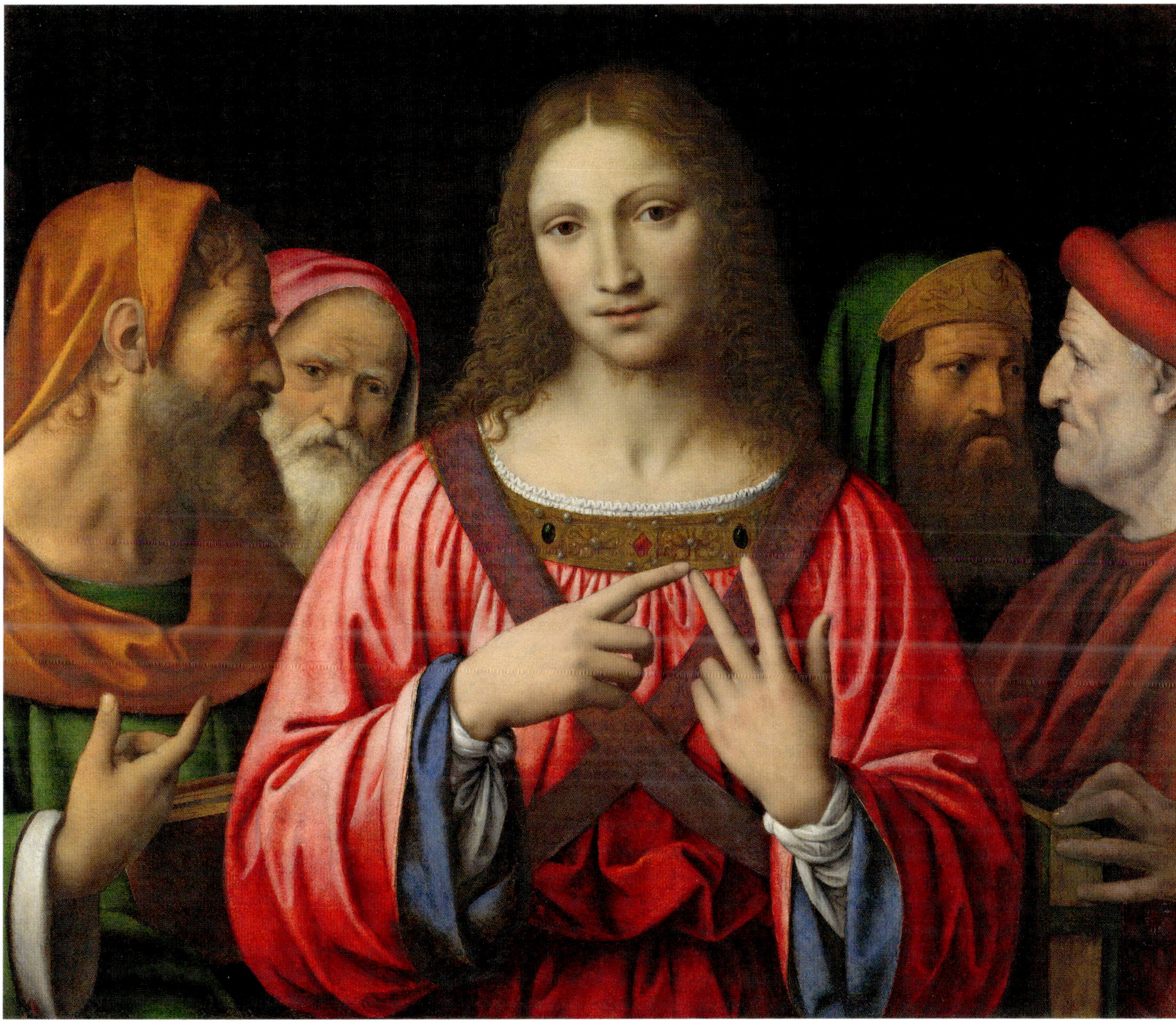

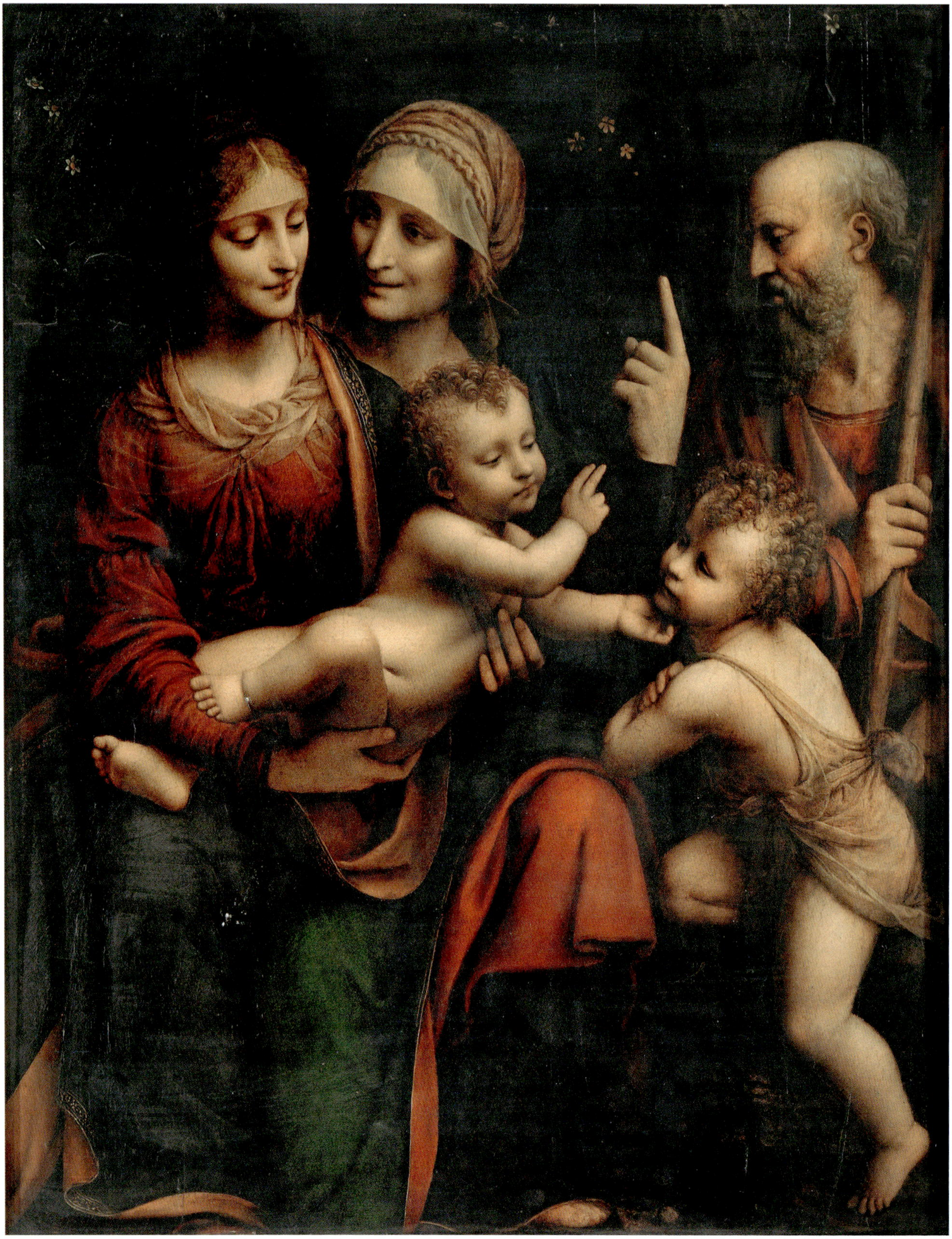

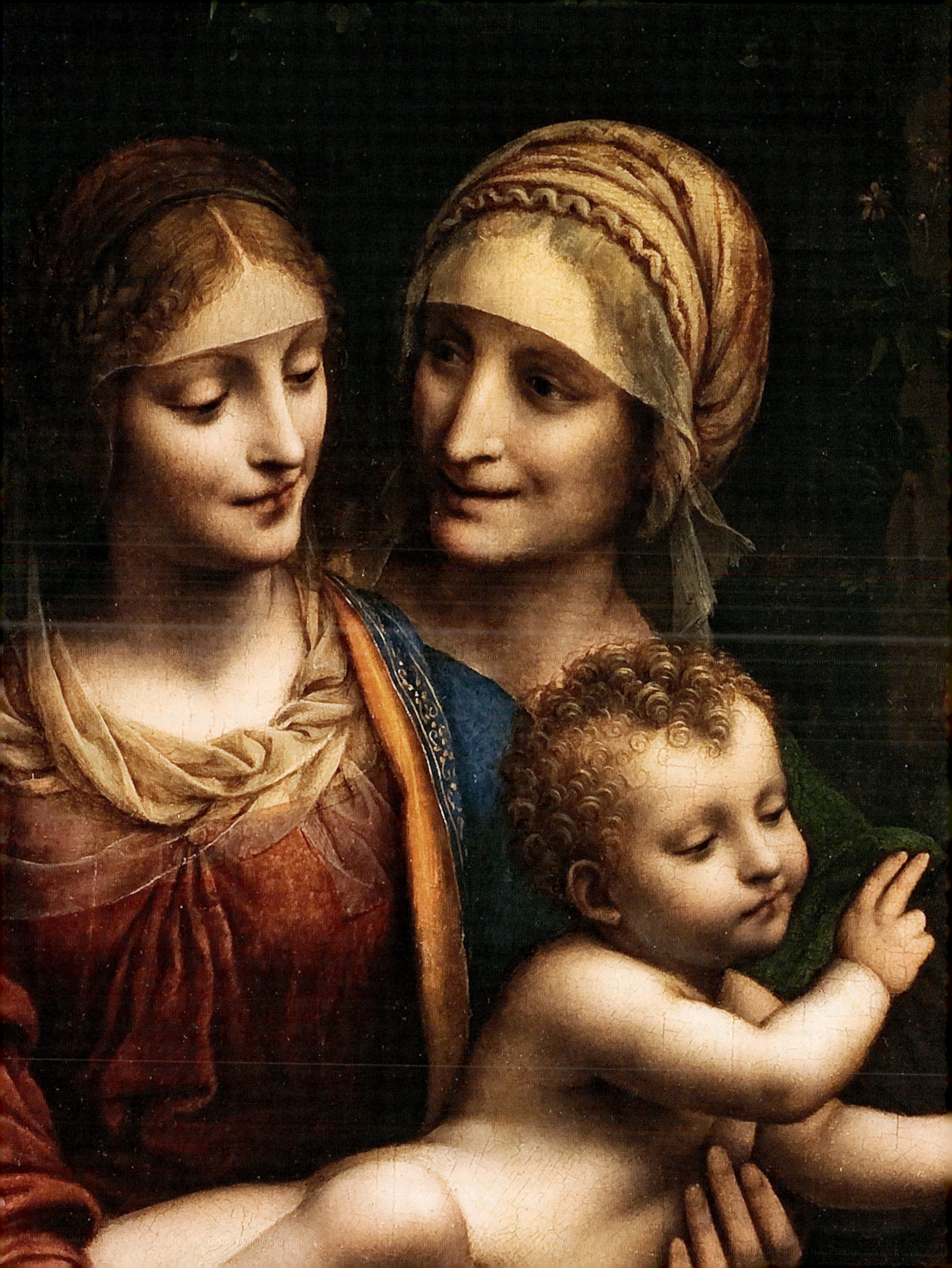

Ambrosiana, were meant to serve as models for contemporary artists and, more broadly, to reform sacred art in accordance with the decrees of the Council of Trent. Borromeo's artistic reform program was promulgated in his *De Pittura Sacra* of 1624, which sets forth his rules on art and its religious function, while his *Musaeum*, published the following year, guided the reader through the works in the museum. Among a number of pictures by or after Luini, the *Holy Family* held pride of place.[78] Borromeo held that in this painting Luini had improved on Leonardo's design by adding a layer of exceptional beauty and tender feeling.[79] The qualities Borromeo sought in art reflected the ideals of the Counter-Reformation, but Luini's work, it should be added, lent itself to his assessment. As Pamela Jones has observed, the artist's "simplification and sweetening of Leonardo's style Borromeo believed had resulted in the creation of particularly effective devotional works."[80]

Though he does not cite the cartoon, it is generally assumed that, by citing Leonardo's draftsmanship, Borromeo meant that Luini took that work as a model for his picture.[81] This may be why he deduced that the younger artist had been Leonardo's pupil. The overall dimensions differ (the cartoon is larger), but the figures are identical in scale, raising the question of how the design was transferred onto the panel. Scientific examination has shown that the outlines in the cartoon were not pricked or indented, so Luini probably resorted to a tracing.[82] Unlike Leonardo's pupils, he drew closer to the recently deceased master in his maturity, spurred on by the opportunity, afforded by Melzi, to turn the cartoon into a painting. As a learning exercise in which Luini sought to master Leonardo's manner, the Ambrosiana picture, which has no known patron, may not have been commissioned at all. Whatever the case, the process of creating it was not simple or straightforward. Unaccustomed as he was to employing contrapposto, Luini doubtless found the complex intertwined poses of the figures challenging. Another difficulty was that many forms in the drawing are unresolved or unfinished, even though it represents the final step in working out the design. To turn such a provisional work into a finished painting, Luini was obliged to complete the sketchily defined forms. Finally, there was the problem of translating the design into a different medium by adding color to Leonardo's gray-toned drawing. Owing to his careful study of the cartoon, Luini's picture displays the exactitude typical of a copy. His attempt to make the cartoon more legible would have appealed to Borromeo, who called for clarity in messaging the content of religious art.

The way it conforms to a model may be what led the curators of the recent exhibition to dismiss Luini's authorship of the Ambrosiana painting in favor of his "eredi," or heirs, meaning his workshop.[83] Their reattribution of the picture to Luini's shop, after his death in 1532, has divided scholars, with the author of the new monograph on the artist in agreement and others opposed.[84] The fame of Borromeo's masterpiece, frequently copied and carried off to Paris during the Napoleonic era, seems deserved, however, though the precise relation between the picture and its source remains to be determined. Executed in tempera and oil on a wood panel, the painting was restored in 2010–11, revealing that it was cut down along the bottom edge, omitting all but one of the females' feet, together with the rocky promontory on which they are seated. Though comparable in size to their counterparts in the cartoon, the figures are consequently larger in scale in relation to the picture area. Among Luini's changes to Leonardo's composition, the most prominent is the addition of Saint Joseph on the right. Bearded and in profile, he is a familiar type in Luini's oeuvre, appearing in the *Lamentation* (fig. 29), for example, and in the predella (fig. 17) of the *Pala Trivulzio*. His inclusion in the Ambrosiana picture is a striking departure from

Fig. 29. Bernardino Luini, *Lamentation over the Dead Christ*, detail of fig. 11

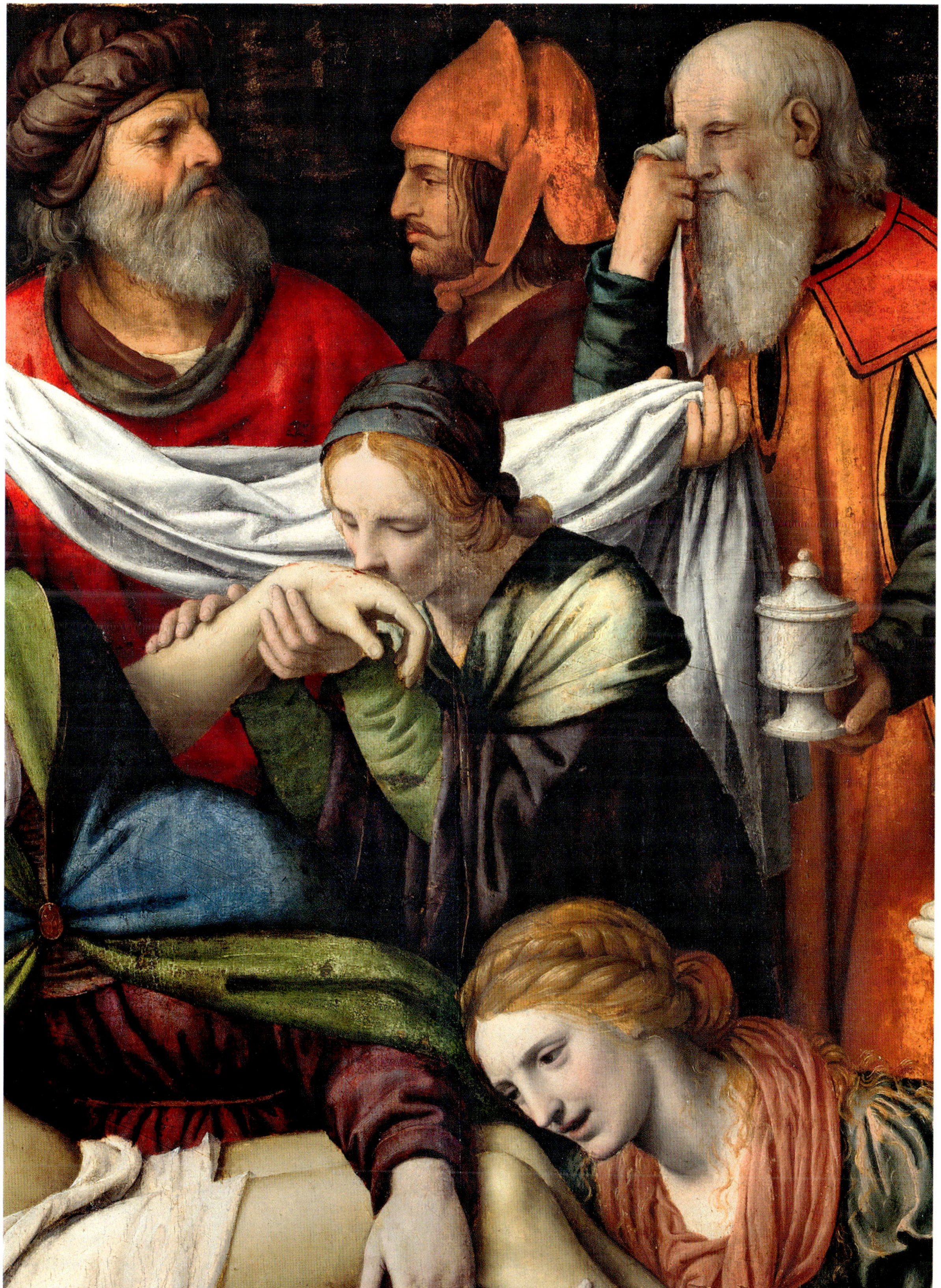

the original, stabilizing the composition and, by turning the subject into a Holy Family, creating a mood of domestic intimacy, both of which served a devotional purpose. Watching over his family, Joseph forms a counterweight to the tightly knit, sculptural group in the cartoon. In addition, Luini altered Leonardo's ambiguous pairing of the two holy women, making Saint Anne older and positioning her clearly behind her daughter. And he clarified their attire as well, adding ocher-colored veils and headdresses and contrasting the red, blue, green, and gold of their garments. The repetition of the warmer hues for Saint Joseph unifies the painting across the surface.

While obviously imitating Leonardo's *chiaroscuro*, Luini's modeling in light and shadow lacks the depth of the original, and there is no evidence for a monochromatic underpainting like that in the *Virgin of the Rocks* (fig. 4). What Luini did borrow from that work was the idea of plants and flowers growing out of rock formations, which Melzi also took over for his *Flora* (fig. 22). Here the dark, shadowy background, setting off the figures, brings them closer to the viewer, as does the cropping of Joseph's figure at right. In this way, the Ambrosiana picture, though lacking the dynamism and mystery of the original, succeeds, nevertheless, in making Leonardo's complex invention accessible.

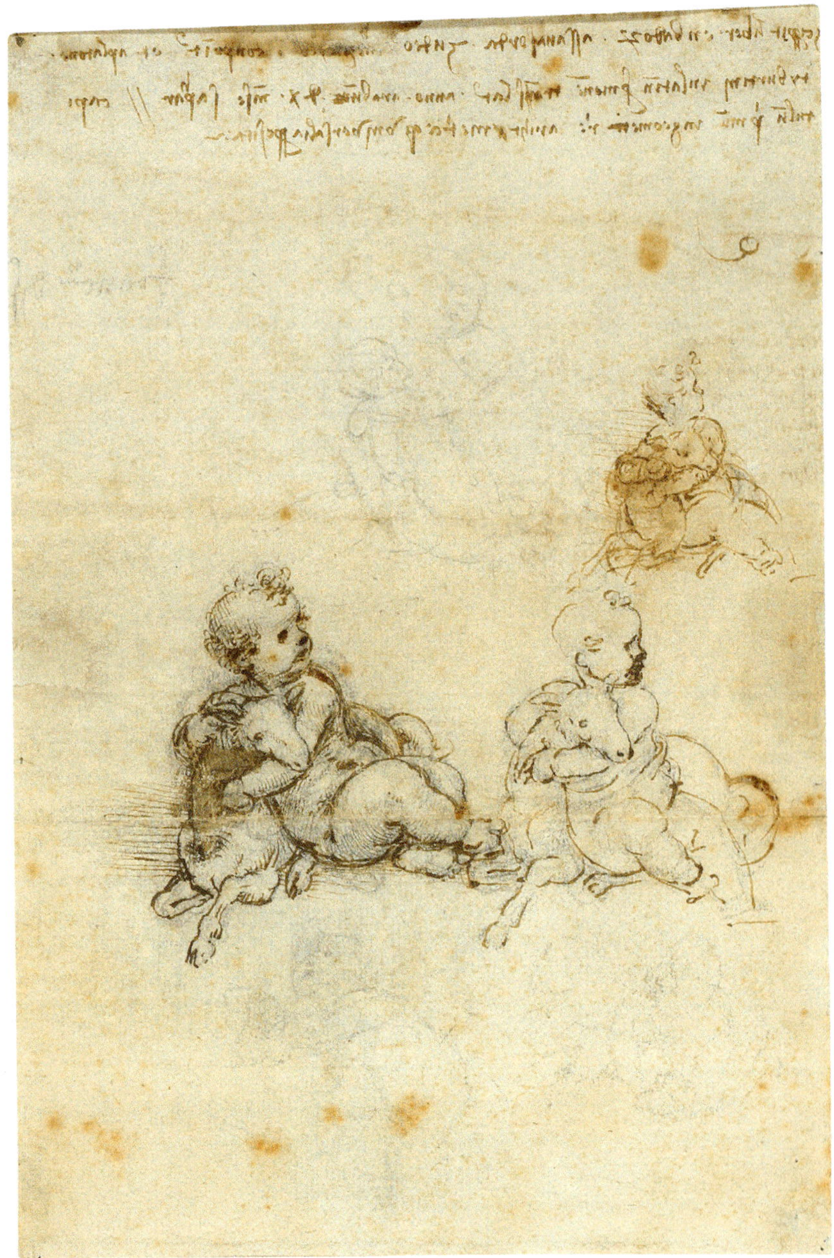

Far from being an isolated exercise, the *Holy Family* became the pivot around which Luini's career as a painter turned. Completed in the early 1520s, the picture is the first in a series of works in which he approached Leonardo more closely.[85] The artist's experience of copying the cartoon demonstrated the potential of Leonardo's art for heightening the efficacy of his own devotional images. And it gave him insights into the master's achievement that he could not have gained by any other method. A related painting by Luini of the *Infant Christ with a Lamb* (fig. 31) was also a favorite of Borromeo's, who donated it to the Ambrosiana in 1618.[86] The motif of the infant holding the sacrificial lamb could have been adapted from Leonardo's *Saint Anne*, as in a fresco by Luini in Lugano.[87] But there the child Christ is standing, whereas he appears to be seated and embracing rather than mounting the lamb, as in the Ambrosiana

Fig. 30. Leonardo da Vinci, *Studies of the Infant Christ Holding a Lamb*, J. Paul Getty Museum, Los Angeles. Detail

Fig. 31. Bernardino Luini, *Infant Christ with a Lamb*, Veneranda Biblioteca Ambrosiana, Milan

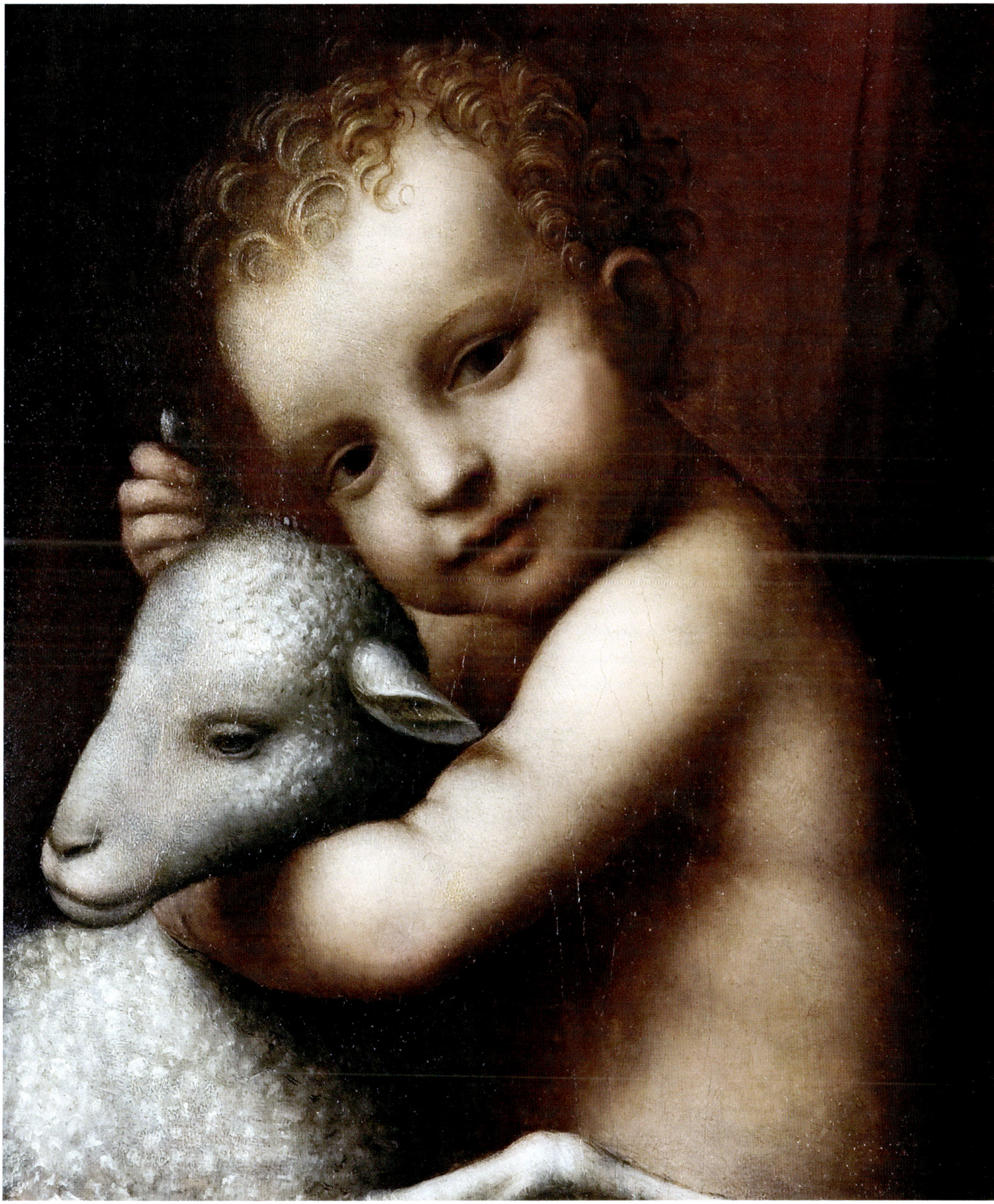

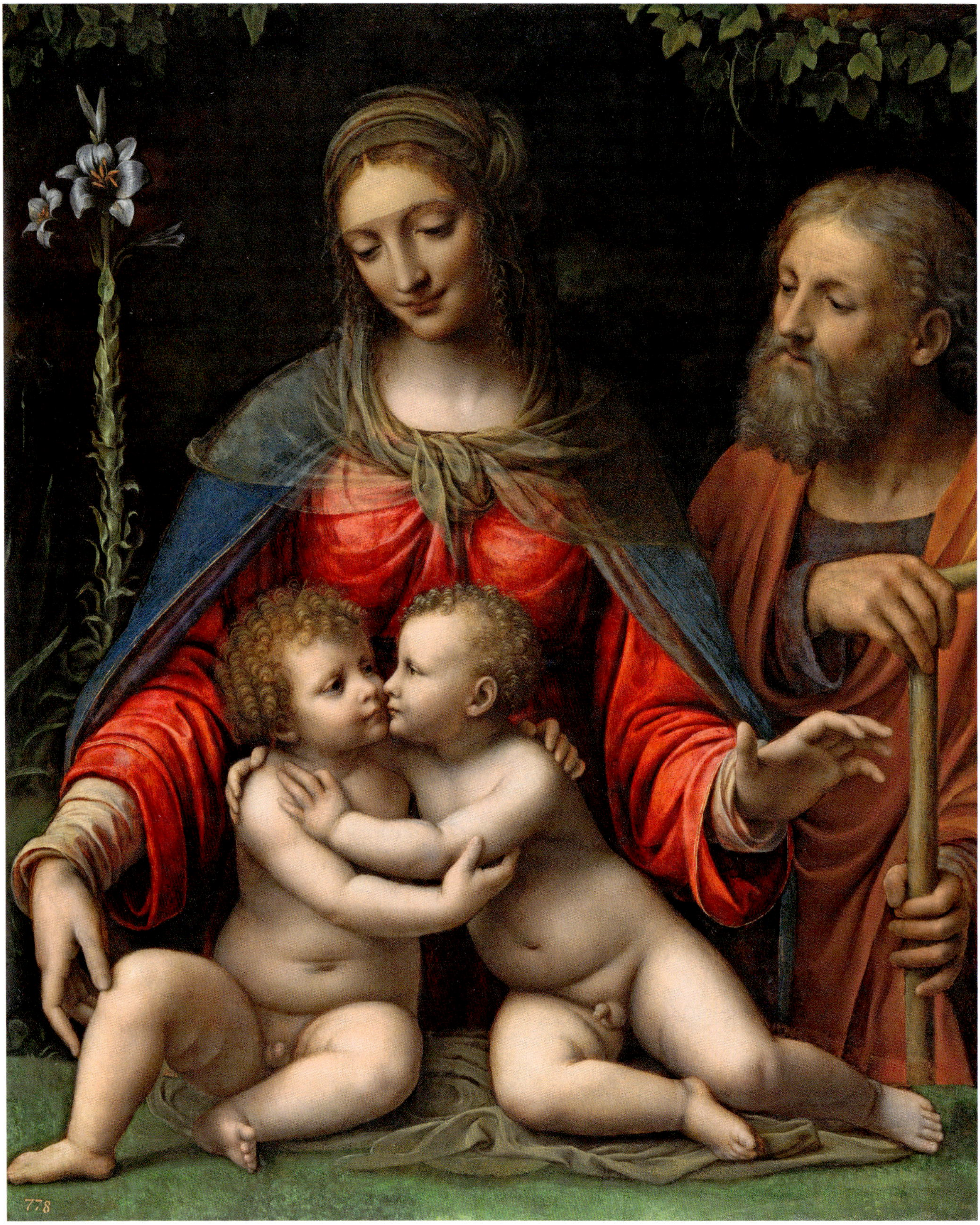
778

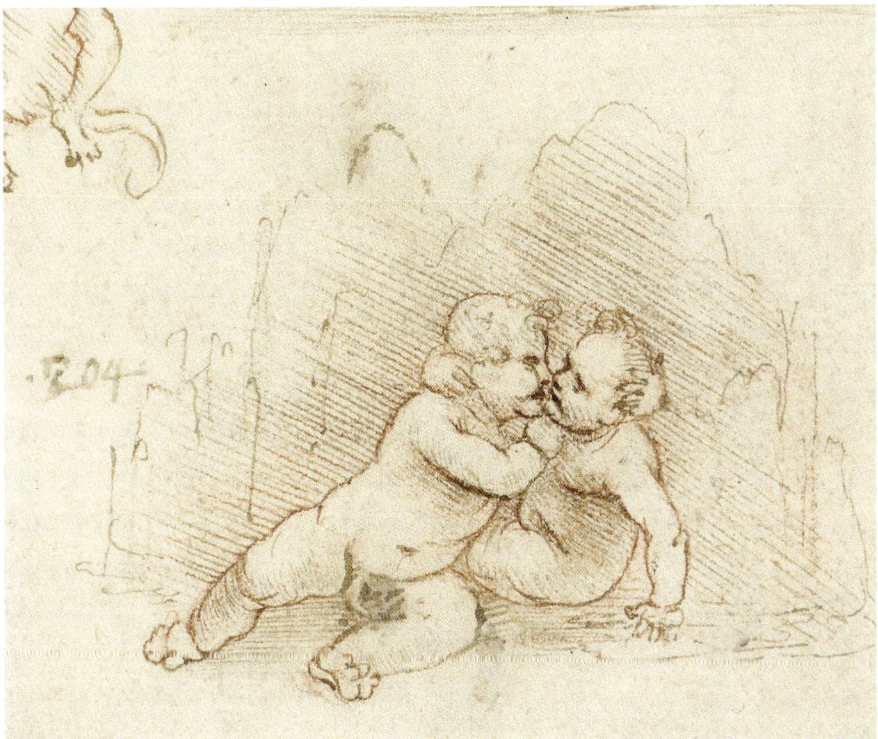

Fig. 32. Bernardino Luini, *Holy Family with the Infant Saint John the Baptist*, Museo Nacional del Prado, Madrid

Fig. 33. Attributed to Leonardo da Vinci, *Two Holy Infants Embracing*, detail, Royal Collection, Windsor Castle

panel. A more likely source for this work is an invention recorded in several drawings in the Getty Museum (fig. 30) and elsewhere, in which Leonardo treated the infant Christ with the lamb as a separate composition.[88] There is no known painting by him of this subject, but the sketches, depicting the recumbent child hugging the lamb's head, may have reached the stage of a cartoon. Luini sharpened the focus in his painting by representing the infant half-length against a dark background. The little Christ, smiling, looks out of the picture which, in a delightful touch borrowed from the *Saint Anne*, shows him grasping the animal's ear as a way of engaging the viewer.

The playful tone of the Ambrosiana picture continues in Luini's *Holy Family with the Infant Saint John the Baptist* (fig. 32) in the Museo del Prado, Madrid.[89] Having acquired the painting as an autograph Leonardo, in 1574 King Philip II placed it in a gallery of religious works at the Escorial, in tacit agreement with Federico Borromeo that the value of a sacred image lay in its devotional function.[90] Dating from the mid-1520s, the Prado panel is Luini's most Leonardesque creation. Like the previous *Holy Family*, it adds the figure of Saint Joseph to a group derived, in this case, from two Leonardo sources – the *Virgin of the Rocks* (fig. 4), and a drawing or painting of the two holy children embracing. Luini was not alone in combining these two models. Another less gifted follower of Leonardo's named Bernardino de' Conti united them in a clumsy pastiche dated 1522, held in the Brera.[91] Here the Virgin is shown full length in a cave-like setting with the children at her feet. Opting to crop the figures, Luini depicts Mary enfolding the infants, who are raised up closer to the viewer. Earlier, in a sketch in the Uffizi, the artist had rendered the theme in a natural "Lombard" manner with the Virgin kneeling and Christ and Saint John reaching across her right leg to embrace each other.[92] Their awkward, if affecting, behavior contrasts with the markedly Leonardesque treatment in Madrid. This work, completed a decade or so after the drawing, has the quality of a demonstration piece in which Luini flaunted his newfound understanding of Leonardo. By now he had clearly fallen under the master's spell.

Luini's depiction of the infants' loving embrace derives from a Leonardo invention known from a sheet at Windsor Castle with various drawings of the Christ Child playing with a cat, which are plainly by a pupil. In the lower right corner a quite different pen-and-ink sketch (fig. 33) represents the infants embracing and kissing in a dark rocky setting. This sketch has also been called a shop product, but it deserves consideration as an autograph work by Leonardo himself.[93] Both infants are nude. The one on the left leans forward while his companion, seated on the right, supports himself as Christ does in the *Virgin of the Rocks*. Judging from the large number of painted copies it inspired north and south of the Alps, Leonardo's design reached the stage of a cartoon or finished painting, in which the

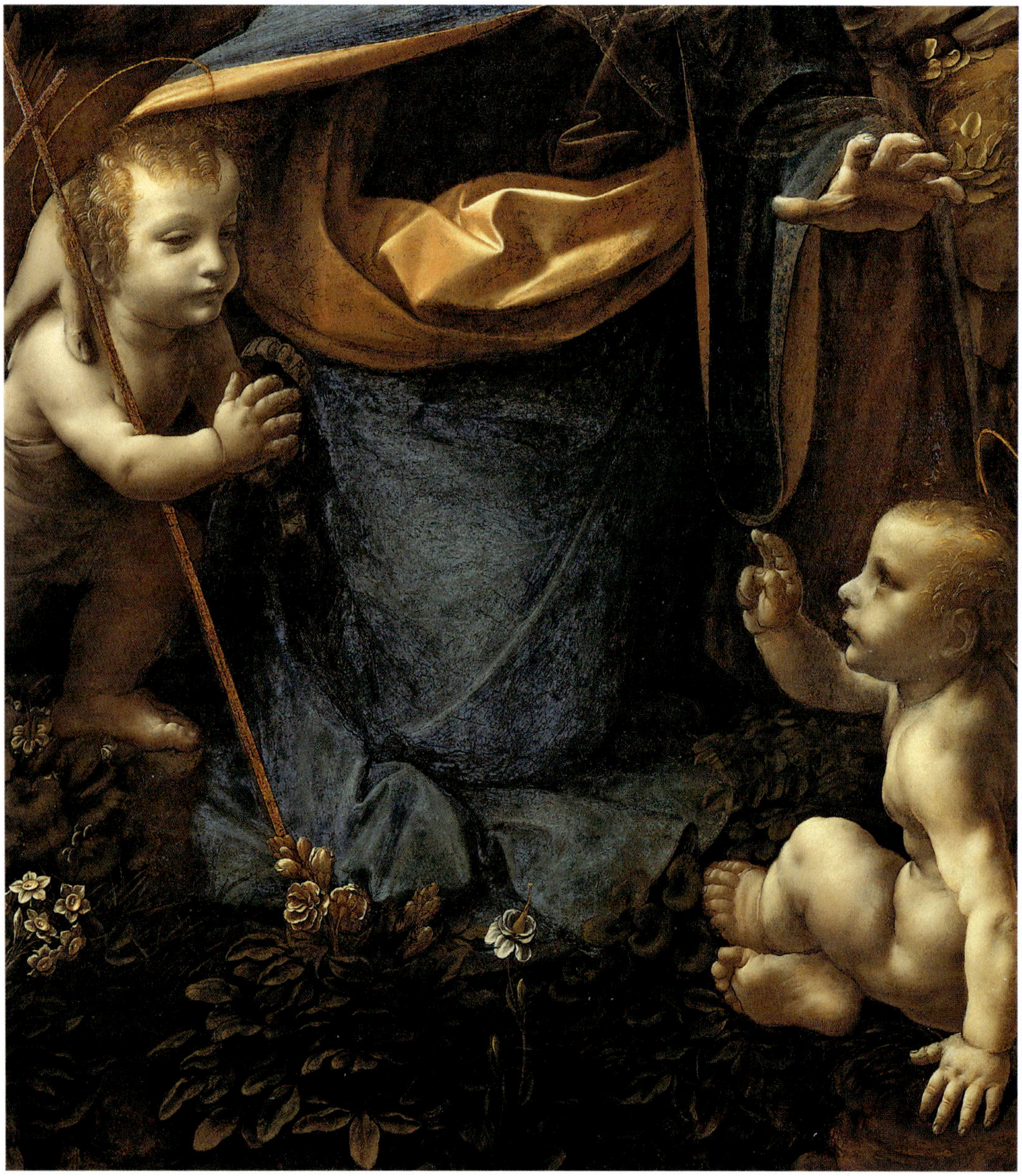

Fig. 34. Leonardo da Vinci, *Virgin of the Rocks*, detail of fig. 4

poses of the infants were reversed.[94] The landscape backgrounds in the copies differ, suggesting that the original was a cartoon of the figures alone, which Melzi may have owned and shown to Luini, whose own full-scale preliminary drawing of the subject is in the École des Beaux-Arts, Paris.[95]

Luini's second source, the *Virgin of the Rocks* (fig. 4), also has as its subject the prophetic meeting of the infants Christ and Saint John (fig. 34). Because their encounter took place on the Holy Family's return from their flight into Egypt, Luini aptly re-introduced Saint Joseph. As in the Ambrosiana picture, his figure, here in three-quarter view, completes the scene of family life in which the believer, devoutly saying his or her prayers, could feel involved. The Virgin's smiling countenance derives from the altarpiece in San Francesco Grande, as do her protective hand gestures, though Luini has modestly veiled Mary's hair.

Likewise, the background in the Prado painting echoes the rocky setting strewn with plants in the *Virgin of the Rocks*. The symbolic lily on the left and ivy on the right also recall the carefully observed plants flanking the protagonist in Melzi's half-length *Flora* (fig. 22). Aside from the delicately rendered vegetation in the Prado picture, Luini's artistry is displayed by the diaphanous veil wound around the Virgin's bust, a bravura bit of skill worthy of Leonardo.

The compositional borrowings, chiaroscuro modeling, and expressive character of the figures bring the Prado panel as close to Leonardo as Luini ever comes. This and the two preceding works follow the same pattern: they all appear to relate to drawings by Leonardo arguably inherited by Melzi, one of which Luini may have owned. In each case, the younger artist painted a picture that Leonardo himself was too busy or distracted to execute. By this time Luini was the most highly accomplished and sought-after painter of devotional images in Lombardy. The artist's *Madonna of the Rose Hedge* (fig. 35), in the Brera, has won recognition as his masterpiece in the genre.[96] Indeed, it is one of the icons of Lombard Renaissance painting. Unlike its predecessors, this picture has no specific model but represents the younger artist's assimilation of Leonardo's manner. Here, Mary recalls her counterpart in the *Virgin of the Rocks*. Seated on a ledge next to a flowerpot, she is veiled, and, like Christ, has no halo. Both figures are strictly frontal. The Virgin does not so much hold her son as display him to the viewer's gaze. Wearing only a transparent shirt, he exchanges glances with the spectator and directs his or her attention to the pot of columbines, symbolizing the Savior's future sacrifice. The infant's interaction with viewer, who completes the scene, contrasts with Luini's depiction of the theme (fig. 36) in the National Gallery of Art, Washington, DC.[97] This work, datable a decade or so before the Brera picture, also depicts the Madonna and Child with a vase of flowers, but it does so in Luini's earlier hybrid mode, treating motifs borrowed from Leonardo in a humbly realistic manner. Lacking volume or presence, the Virgin looks girlish, and the clothed Child is absorbed with the flower. Their haloes shine against the dark background. The Brera Madonna is altogether more artful, not only in the figures but in the trellis intertwined with pink and white roses directly behind them. The rose hedge alludes to the traditional iconography of the *hortus conclusus*, or enclosed garden, symbolic of the Virgin's purity. Like the columbines, the roses are a stimulus to meditation, while closing off the background in the manner of the plant-strewn rocks in the *Holy Families*. Here, however, the greenery does not darken the space. Nor does it mute the artist's palette, which, in its colorful array of pink, yellow, and blue, resembles his aforementioned frescos at Saronno.

Leonardo's influence on Luini extended beyond religious paintings to include portraiture. The younger artist's frescos and altarpieces contain numerous portraits of donors kneeling in profile. But the *Portrait of a Lady* (fig. 37), also in the National Gallery of Art, is his only certain independent likeness.[98] Here Luini's newly acquired Leonardesque style was used not to reinforce a devotional message, but to portray the sitter. The unidentified young woman, depicted half-length and lifesize, faces the viewer. Wearing an elaborate costume indicative of her high social status, she fingers a gold chain and holds a fur piece. Green curtains framing the dark background provide the same kind of semi-enclosed setting as the rose hedge in the Brera Madonna. Rare as it is, the Washington picture is also one of the few works by Luini to have been scientifically investigated. Carried out in connection with the conservation treatment of 2014, the examination revealed that Luini, by contrast to Leonardo, used a "spare technique, employing thin films of paint applied in only a few – sometimes only two – layers."[99] And he

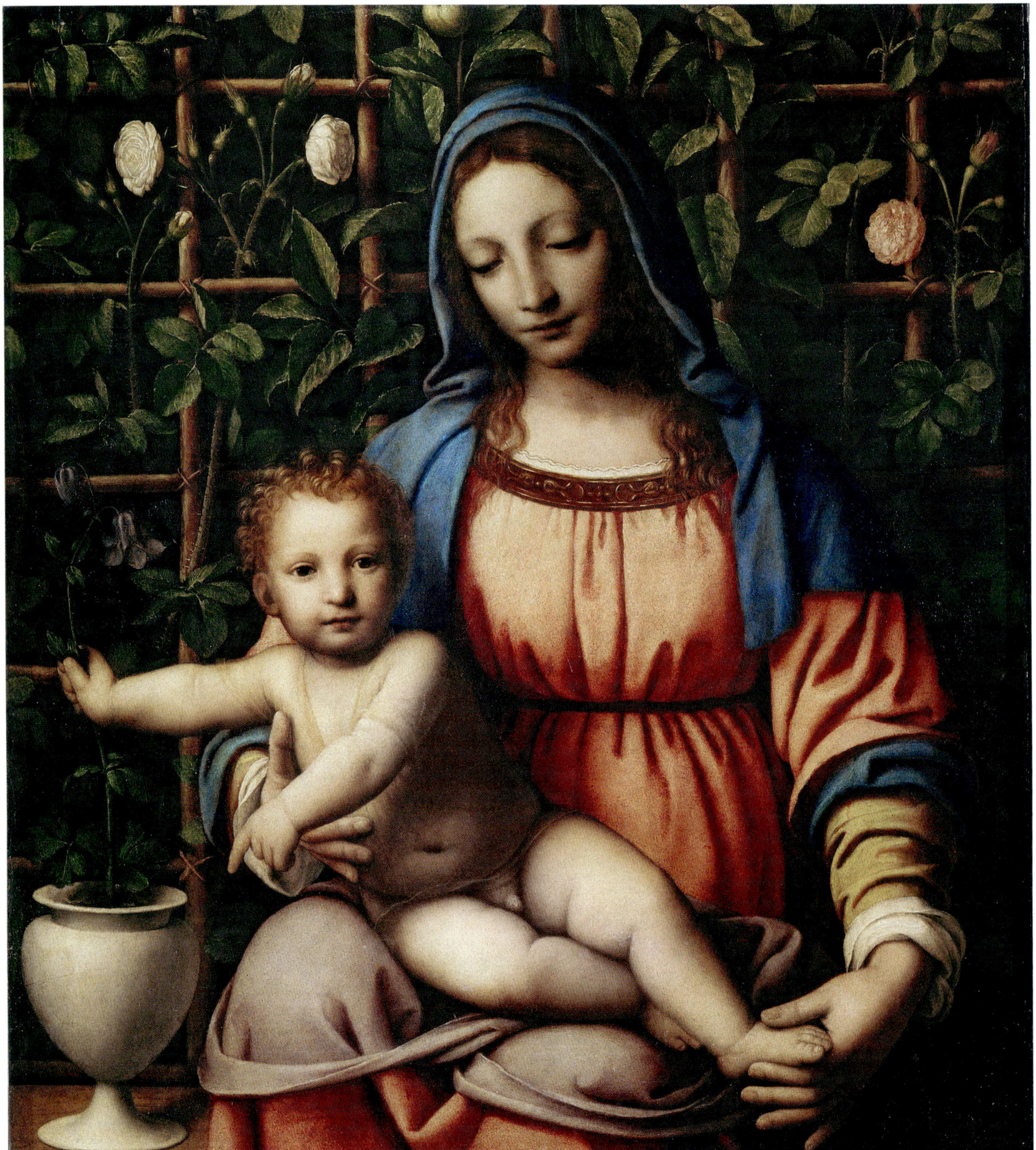

Fig. 35. Bernardino Luini, *Madonna of the Rose Hedge*, Pinacoteca di Brera, Milan

Fig. 36. Bernardino Luini, *Virgin and Child*, Samuel H. Kress Collection, National Gallery of Art, Washington, DC

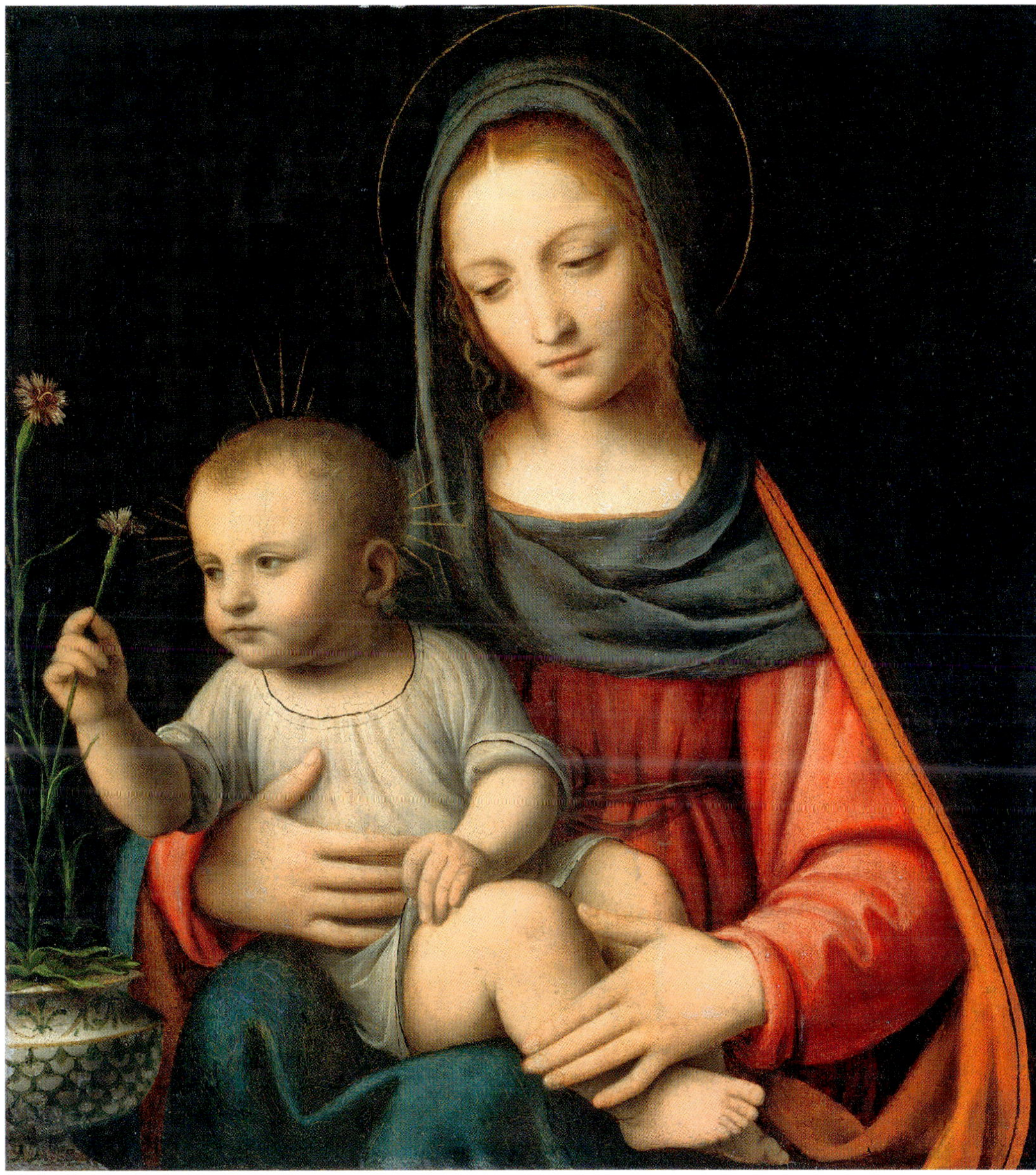

painted the flesh tones directly on the gesso ground of his panel, using darker oil glazes for the shadows. Infrared reflectography further showed that the underdrawing beneath the paint surface is rudimentary, limited to the outlines of forms.

The concept underlying the portrait is anything but simple, however. The psychology of the sitter – her "Leonardo smile" – has been traced to *Mona Lisa* (fig. 38).[100] Long before it became the most famous painting in the world, Leonardo's dynamic image of a woman turning to confront the viewer was taken as a model by other artists, especially in Florence, where Leonardo first began the portrait. Luini, in Milan, evidently recalled the original or knew it in the form of a copy, like one in the Prado.[101] He might even have seen a (lost) preliminary cartoon belonging to Melzi. To characterize his sitter, Leonardo lent her the distinctive facial type and smiling expression he adopted for Saint Anne (fig. 8). In other words, he imposed an ideal type on the features of an individual. As an idealized portrait, *Mona Lisa* does not convey the sitter's actual character or appearance, which remain unknown. Following Leonardo, Luini portrays his subject according to an ideal of female beauty shared with his other works of the 1520s. The sitter bears a "family resemblance" to the artist's *Flora* (fig. 23), for example, as well as his Madonnas and saints. As a female portrait, the Washington picture is joined by Luini's lovely study of a woman holding a fan, in the Albertina, Vienna.[102] Executed in a mixed technique of black and colored chalks, this work is similar in format to the *Lady*, but here the fashionably dressed sitter is presented realistically, in her own character and features.

Leonardo had pioneered the use of colored chalks for portraiture in his cartoon for a likeness of Isabella d'Este, of 1500, in the Louvre.[103] And Isabella herself was a model for the ball-shaped headdress worn by Luini's lady in Washington. Placed atop smoothly combed hair parted in the middle, the *balzo* or *capigliara*, as it was called, differs from Mona Lisa's veil.[104] As the wife of a Florentine merchant, Leonardo's sitter is soberly dressed in attire that would not have suited a high-born Italian woman in the 1520s. Luini's solitary portrait belongs, in fact, to a series of aristocratic images of women painted in various centers throughout the peninsula.[105] His subject wears a black dress with puffy, balloon-like sleeves, worn over a chemise with a cream-colored partlet. And she holds a *zibellino*, or pelt of a marten, as an accessory. The artist's treatment of this sartorial finery looks restrained, however, compared with Solario's contemporary *Portrait of a Lady* (fig. 39), in the Galleria Nazionale, Palazzo Barberini, Rome.[106] As sequels to *Mona Lisa*, both portraits go back to Leonardo but in different ways. Like him, Solario shows his sitter rotating in a chair, but her face is her own, bearing no resemblance to Andrea's Madonnas. Choosing to typecast his sitter, Luini focused on Lisa's physiognomy rather than her pose. Both artists depict their female subjects in the latest fashion, but while Solario lavishes attention on the lady's opulent red and green costume, Luini renders a similar outfit with his usual economy of means.

Luini's conversion to a Leonardesque manner was based on his study of more than one of the master's works, certainly, yet Leonardo provided no model for the so-called *Sacra Conversazione*. This type of altarpiece featured the Virgin and Child surrounded by saints, and was often divided into separate sections. Leonardo had declined to paint such a polyptych, or multi-paneled altarpiece, for San Francesco Grande, instead producing the *Virgin of the Rocks* (fig. 4), in which the principals appear in a single, unified space. Forty years later, in 1523, Luini was commissioned to paint a polyptych for the high altar of the Bramantesque basilica of San Magno in Legnano near

Fig. 37. Bernardino Luini, *Portrait of a Lady*, Andrew W. Mellon Collection, National Gallery of Art, Washington, DC

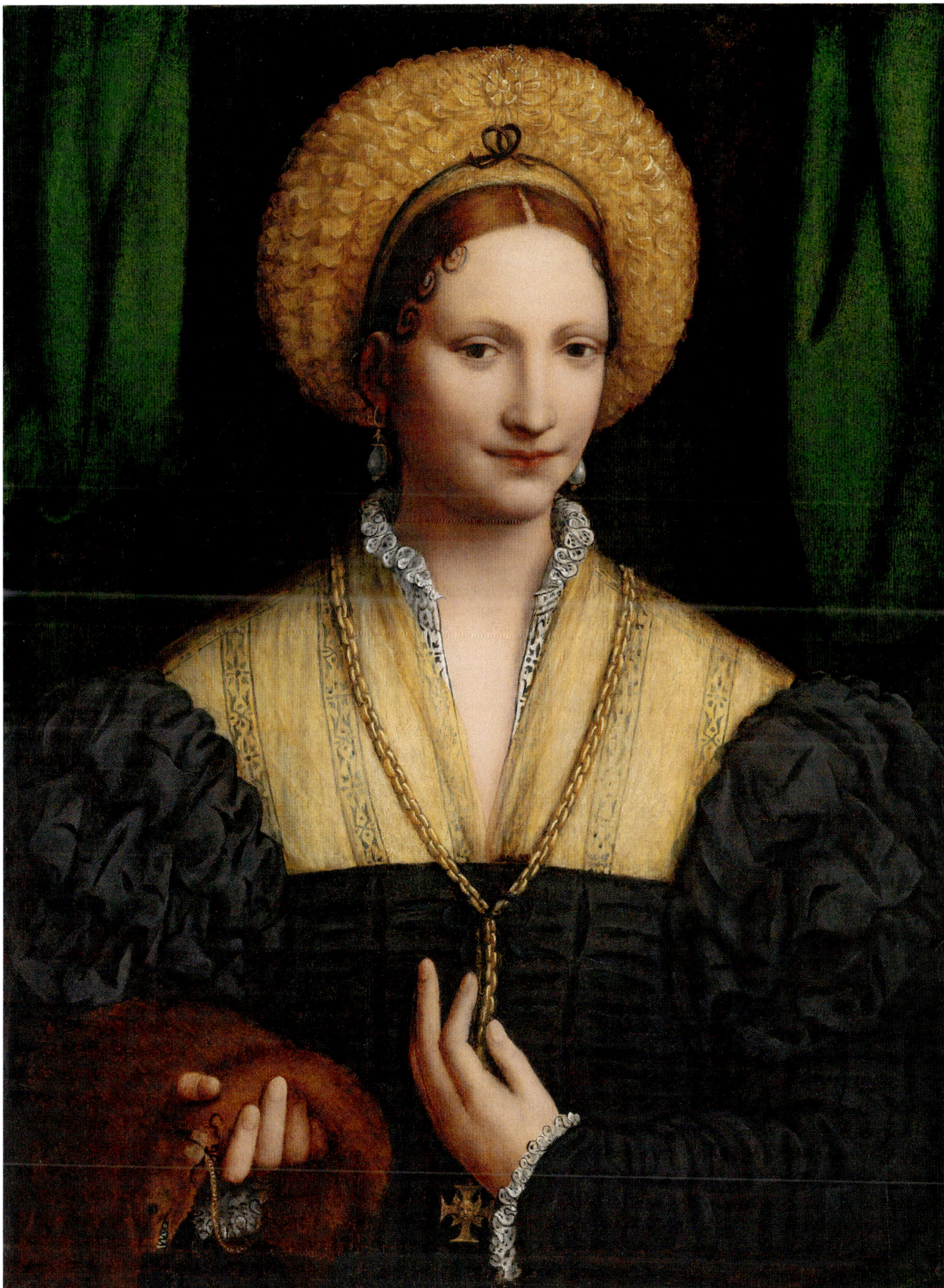

Milan. Still in situ, this imposing work (fig. 40) is arranged in three tiers with saints, one atop another, flanking a large central panel depicting the Virgin and Child enthroned with angels, surmounted by a pediment portraying God the Fathcer.[107] The monochrome predella has scenes from Christ's Passion. In fulfilling the commission, Luini's problem was how to adapt the lesson he had learned from Leonardo to the more traditional format prescribed by his patrons. To organize his composition, he had the elaborate architectural setting for the figures repeat that of the frame and continue from one compartment to another. The saints, shown kneeling in the lateral panels, link the Virgin and Child with the viewer by means of gesture and glance. The strategy of posing the saints in attitudes reminiscent of Leonardo's kneeling angel makes the altarpiece spatially comprehensible. The lively poses of the music-making angels, along with that of the infant Christ holding a globe, contrast with the Virgin's posture, which harks back to the formality of earlier Lombard art. Mary's facial type and sweet, smiling expression, on the other hand, specifically recall Leonardo's Saint Anne (fig. 8) in the Louvre. The expressive mode of the figures, combined with their intense realism, suggests that Luini, commissioned to paint an altarpiece, restudied Leonardo's in San Francesco Grande.[108] In that instance, the master had spotlighted the protagonists in a grotto-like setting, reducing color in favor of an overall tonal scheme. Luini similarly unifies the separate elements of his polyptych by means of a darkened ambient. And he models the figures with depth and precision: as in the Prado *Holy Family*, they have a pronounced three-dimensionality. With the actors brought up close to the surface, Luini's version of Leonardo's chiaroscuro combines with the rich coloration of their garments and the gilded frame to create, on a grand scale, a sumptuous effect unmatched in Lombard painting. His solution to the problem of how to paint a Leonardesque altarpiece found favor, inspiring numerous partial copies, including one that belonged to Federico Borromeo.

The works by Luini that we have just examined consist of half-length devotional panels for private use, together with a portrait and an altarpiece, all with dark backgrounds, dating to the 1520s. This group could be expanded to include other such Leonardesque productions, like the artist's *Saint Catherine with Angels* in the Hermitage or his Madonna at Capodimonte in Naples.[109] But what about Leonardo's relevance for paintings by Luini that do not fall into this category? In frescos, like his *Last Supper* at Lugano or the *Salvator Mundi* in the Louvre, the master's influence is limited to facial types and motifs, as the medium was unsuited to chiaroscuro.[110] In other examples, Luini's adaptations from Leonardo are ingenious, like this half-length depiction (fig. 41), turning the angel in the *Virgin of the Rocks* into the reluctant Joseph fleeing Potiphar's wife, in the Duke of Wellington Collection at Apsley House, London.[111] By this time his use of Leonardo models had grown confident and assured. The final stage of his involvement with Leonardo is represented by the *Virgin and Child with the Infant Saint John and a Lamb* in the Museo Thyssen-Bornemisza, Madrid (fig. 42).[112] Numerous copies of the work attest to the high esteem in which it was held. In it Luini returns to the subject of his earlier fresco (fig. 9) in the Museo Nazionale della Scienza in Milan. There the derivations from Leonardo's own versions of the theme, however specific, lack cogency or grace. The holy figures and the lamb are stiffly posed and loosely grouped, in the Lombard manner. The Thyssen treatment of the theme is more ambitious, both in imitating Leonardo and in its appeal to the viewer. The figure of the Christ Child reaching out toward the lamb is simply reversed from the fresco, but his companion here bends over and lowers the animal to the reverently kneeling position found in Leonardo's original. In all these works, as in Luini's Ambrosiana picture (fig. 31), Christ grasps the lamb by the ear. Also shown kneeling, the sweetly smiling Virgin

Fig. 38. Leonardo da Vinci, *Mona Lisa*, Musée du Louvre, Paris

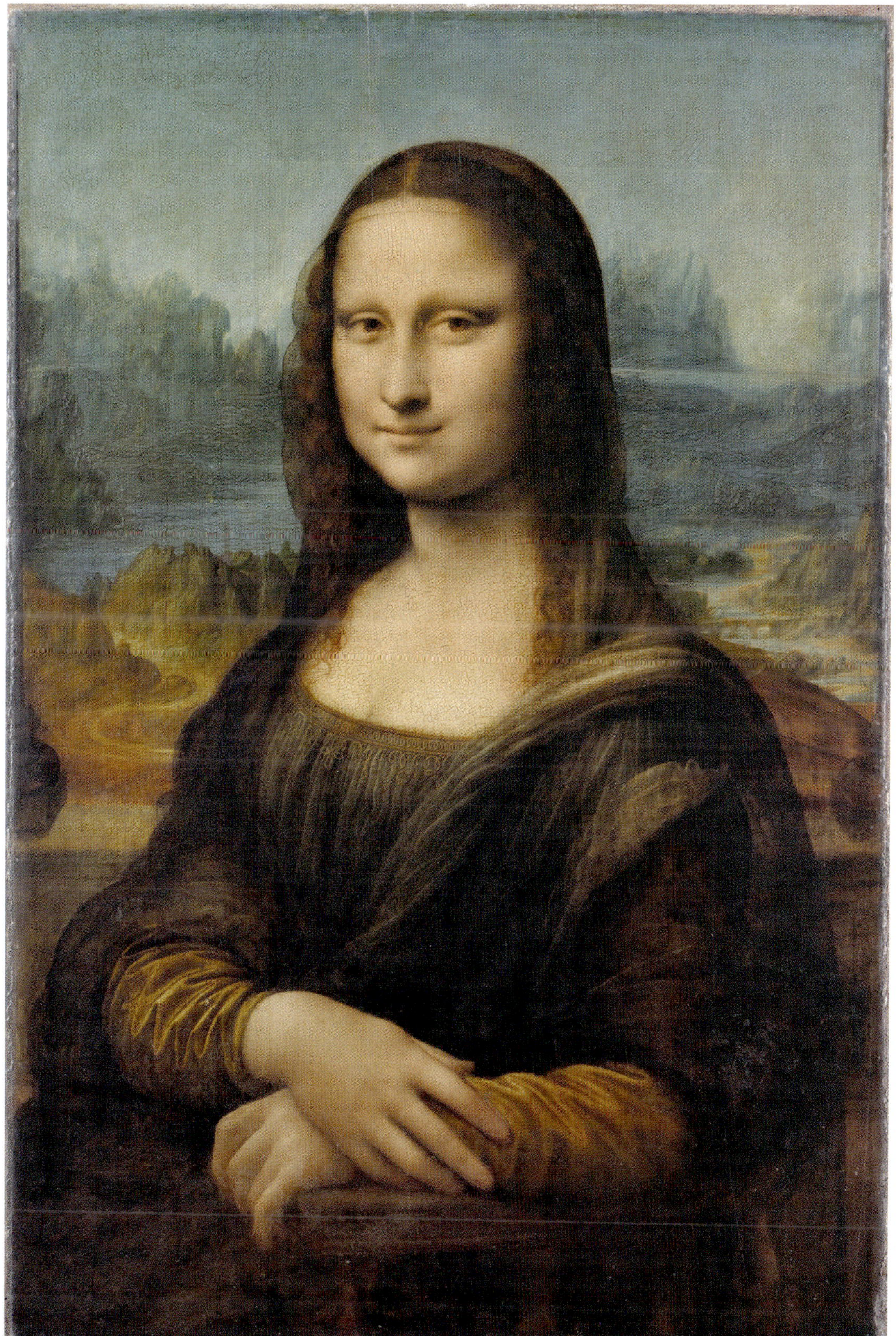

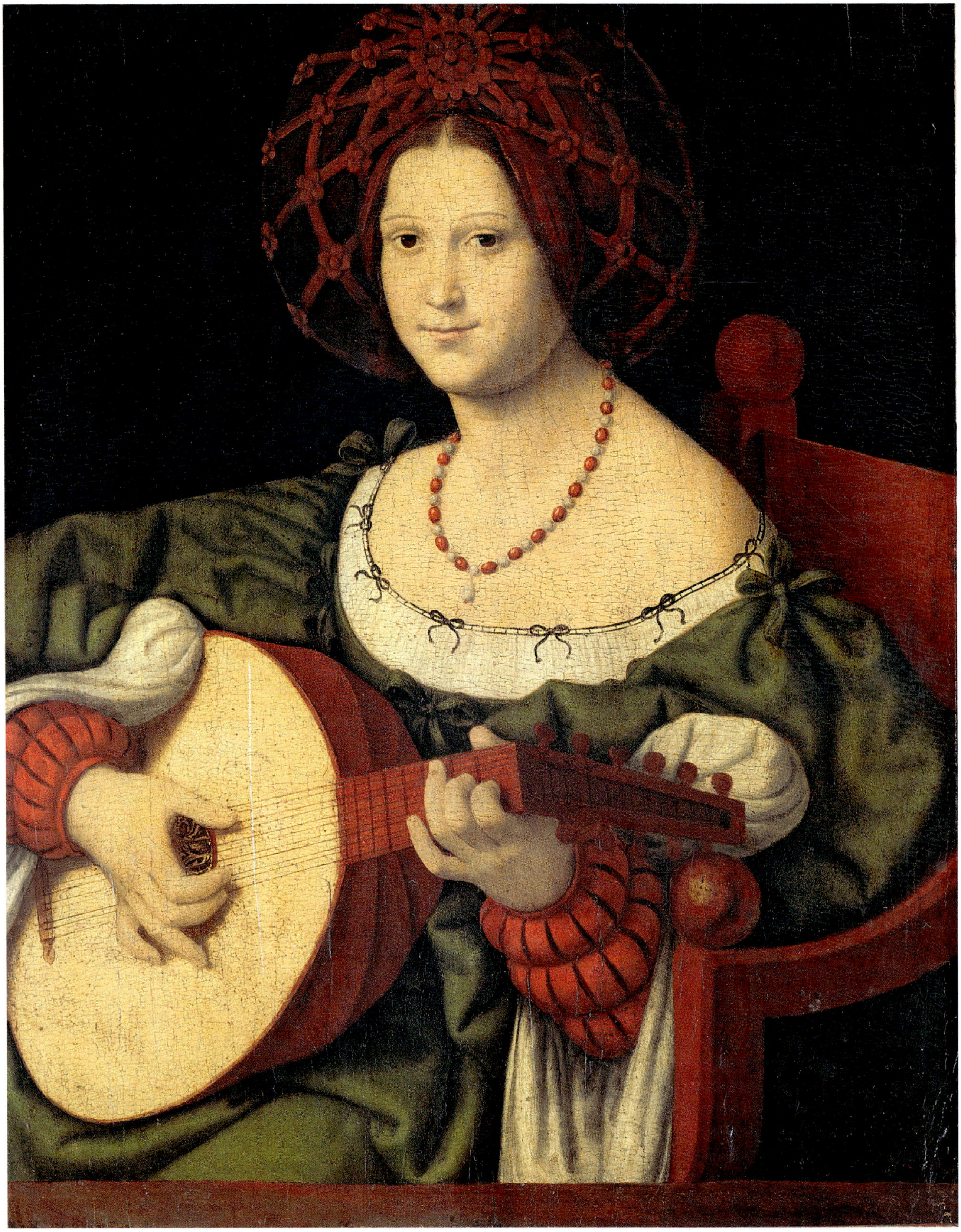

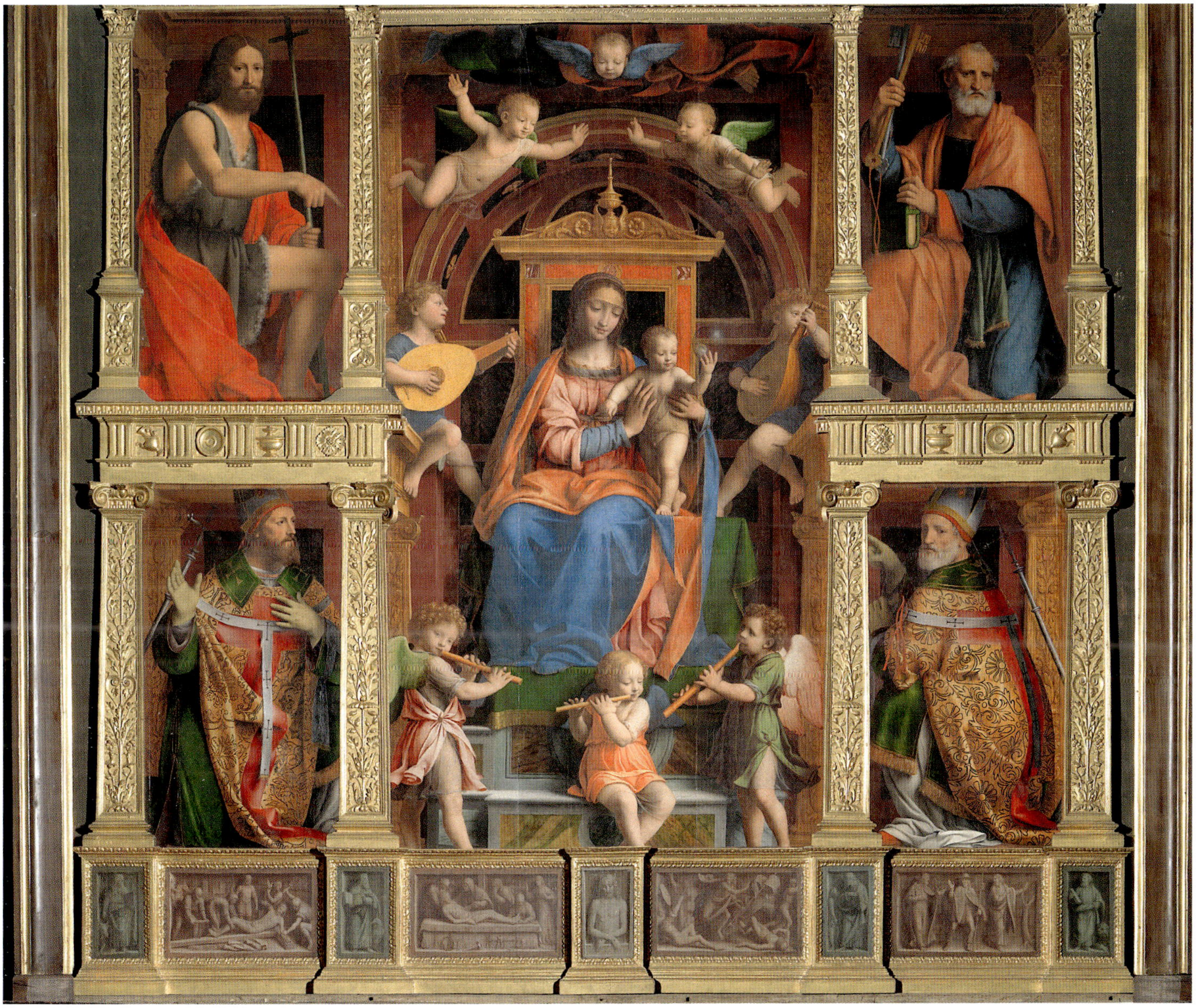

Fig. 39. Andrea Solario, *Portrait of a Lady*, Galleria Nazionale d'Arte Antica, Palazzo Barberini, Rome

Fig. 40. Bernardino Luini, *Virgin and Child Enthroned with Saints and Angels*, Basilica dei Santi Salvatore e Magno, Legnano (Milan)

bends solicitously over the children. Though none of them echoes Leonardo exactly, the figures form a compact unity and together reflect their "moti dell'anima," or inner feelings, in pose and expression. Charged with emotion, the scene is set in a rocky enclosure before a landscape full of human activity, as in the fresco, but with distant mountains in the background. Luini's mastery of Leonardo's idiom, based on a closer familiarity with it, was now as complete as could be desired. And yet, for all its mature artistry, the Thyssen picture still preserves the simplicity and directness that Luini always sought in his work. Looking at Leonardo through his eyes, we come to understand how this gifted follower approached the master not out of slavish imitation, but with his own goals in mind. Borromeo realized that Luini was first and foremost a devotional artist who looked to aid the faithful in their image-based prayers. Standing or kneeling in front of his paintings, the viewer could feel emotionally and spiritually connected to their subjects. And this dialogue continues to the present day.

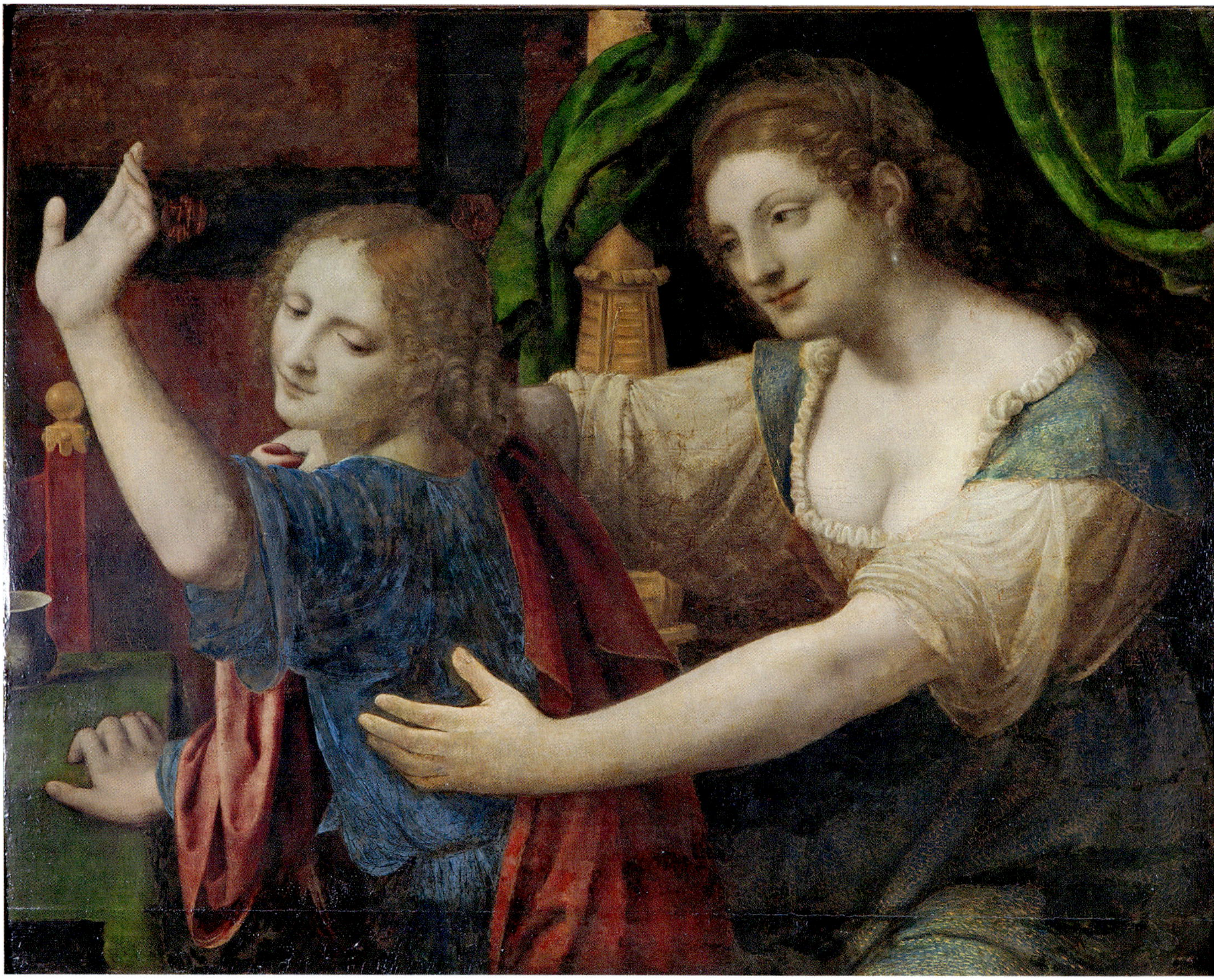

Fig. 41. Bernardino Luini, *Joseph and Potiphar's Wife*, The Wellington Collection, Apsley House, London

[1] The relation between form and function in Christian devotional art is explored in three exhibition catalogues: Henk van Os, *The Art of Devotion in the Late Middle Ages in Europe 1300–1500*, Princeton, 1994; "*The Image of Christ*, accompanying the exhibition 'Seeing Salvation'," ed. Gabriele Finaldi, London, 2000; and *Pious Journeys. Christian Devotional Art and Practice in the Later Middle Ages and Renaissance*, ed. Linda Seidel, Chicago, 2001. Most of the literature deals with the Middle Ages and the Counter-Reformation, that is, before and after the period that concerns us here.

[2] Giorgio Vasari, *Le Vite de più Eccellenti Pittori Scultori ed Architettori*, ed. Gaetano Milanesi, 9 vols., Florence, 1878–85, vol. IV, 1879, p. 585; and vol. V, 1880, pp. 519–20. For a comprehensive account of Luini's critical fortune, see Cristina Quattrini, *Bernardino Luini*, Milan, 2019, pp. 6–25.

[3] Giovanni Paolo Lomazzo, *Scritti sull'arte*, ed. Roberto Paolo Ciardi, 2 vols., Florence, 1973–75.

[4] Luigi Lanzi, *Storia Pittorica della Italia dal Risorgimento delle Belle Arti fin presso la Fine del XVIII Secolo* (orig. ed. Bassano, 1795–96), ed. Martino Capucci, 3 vols., Florence, 1968–74, vol. II, 1970, pp. 310–13. The idea going back to Lanzi that Luini portrayed himself and Leonardo as bearded old men in one of the Saronno frescos is fanciful, as these are generic types.

[5] Franz Theodor Kugler, *Handbook of Painting. The Italian* Schools (orig. German ed. Berlin, 1837), ed. Charles Lock Eastlake, 2 vols., London, 1869, vol. II, pp. 291–93; and Alexis-François Rio, *Leonardo da Vinci e la sua Scuola* (orig. French ed. Paris, 1855), trans. V. G. De Castro, Milan, 1856, pp. 127–36.

[6] John Christian, "Burne-Jones's Second Italian Journey," in *Apollo*, vol. CII, no. 165, November 1975, pp. 334–37; and Colin Harrison and Christopher Newall, *The Pre-Raphaelites and Italy* (exh. Ashmolean Museum), Oxford, 2010, cat. 52, pp. 100–1.

[7] John Ruskin, The *Cestus of Aglaia*, 1865–66, in *The Works of John Ruskin*, eds. E. T. Cook and A. Wedderburn, 39 vols., London, 1903–12, vol. XIX, 1905, pp. 130–31.

[8] *Works*, eds. Cook and Wedderburn, vol. XXI, 1906, p. 125.

[9] *Illustrated Catalogue of Pictures by Masters of the Milanese and Allied Schools of Lombardy* (exh. Burlington Fine Arts Club, 1898), ed. Herbert Cook, London, 1899; and George C. Williamson, *Bernardino Luini*, London, 1899.

[10] Bernard Berenson, *North Italian Painters of the Renaissance*, New York & London, 1907, pp. 108, 117–19. Echoing this view is Sydney J. Freedberg, *Painting in Italy 1500 to 1600*, Pelican History of Art Series, Harmondsworth, 1971, pp. 264–65.

[11] Adolfo Venturi, *Storia dell'Arte Italiana. IX. La Pittura del Cinquecento. Parte II*, Milan, 1926, pp. 753, 763–68.

[12] Luca Beltrami, *Bernardino Luini 1512–1532. Materiale di Studio*, Milan, 1911.

[13] Angela Ottino Della Chiesa, *Bernardino Luini*, Novara, 1956, pp. 48–53. Three years earlier the author organized an exhibition devoted to Luini in Como. Roberto Longhi (*Officina Ferrarese, 1934. Seguito dagli Ampliamenti 1940 e dai Nuovi Ampliamenti 1940–55*, Florence, 1956, pp. 123–71) similarly saw Luini as a Lombard precursor of Caravaggio's naturalism.

[14] Maria Teresa Binaghi Olivari, *Bernardino Luini*, Milan 2007, citing her specialized contributions relating Luini to the religious reform, inspired by the semi-heretical *Apocalypsis Nova* of the Franciscan Amadeo Mendez da Silva, in early sixteenth-century Milan. Her broad notion of the movement's influence (pp. 17–19) has been re-dimensioned by later scholarship to include only the iconography of a few specific works, like the Saint Joseph fresco cycle in the Brera (Quattrini, *Luini*, 2019, cat. 26, pp. 174–83).

[15] *Bernardino Luini e i suoi figli* (exh. Palazzo Reale, Milan), eds. Giovanni Agosti and Jacopo Stoppa, 2 vols., Milan, 2014; and Quattrini, *Luini*, 2019. Further on Luini see Giulio Bora, "Bernardino Luini," in *The Legacy of Leonardo. Painters in Lombardy 1490–1530*, eds. Giulio Bora, Maria Teresa Fiorio, Pietro C. Marani, and Janice Shell, Milan, 1998, pp. 325–70.

[16] Maria Cecilia Cavallone, Giacomo Giannelli, and Egon Tagliabue in *Luini*, eds. Agosti and Stoppa, 2014, vol. 2, cat. 4, pp. 39–41; and Quattrini, *Luini*, 2019, cat. 17, pp. 146–47.

[17] For the tradition of Lombard naturalism see: Andrea Bayer, "Defining Naturalism in Lombard Painting," in *Painters of Reality. The Legacy of Leonardo and Caravaggio in Lombardy* (exh. Metropolitan Museum of Art), ed. Andrea Bayer, New York, 2004, pp. 2–19; and Nicholas Hall and Virginia Brilliant, *Faithful to Nature. Eleven Lombard Paintings 1530–1760*, New York, 2019.

[18] The literature on the two versions of the *Virgin of the Rocks* is interminable. See Luke Syson in *Leonardo da Vinci. Painter at the Court of Milan* (exh. National Gallery), eds. Luke Syson and Larry Keith, London, 2011, pp. 160–75. The remarks that follow reprise the discussion in David Alan Brown, *Leonardo da Vinci. Art and Devotion in the Madonnas of his Pupils*, Cinisello Balsamo (Milan), 2003, pp. 43–48.

[19] Edoardo Villata, *Leonardo da Vinci. I Documenti e le Testimonianze Contemporanee*, Milan, 1999, no. 67, pp. 72–73: "*che* dicti Scolari non sono in talibus experti et quod cechus non iudicat de colore."

[20] The technical examination and treatment of the *Virgin of the Rocks* (see the following note) demonstrated that Leonardo laid in the tonal underpainting and completed much of the picture in the 1490s, then put on the finishing touches between 1506 and 1508. The execution of the figures appears largely autograph, but the landscape setting plainly lacks the geological and botanical accuracy of the rock formations and plants in the Louvre version. While certain details like the heads of the Virgin and the angel are clearly superior to pupils' work, who assisted the master is difficult to say. Formerly, Leonardo's helper was taken to be Ambrogio de Predis, who was credited with most or all of the painting. The only part of the *ancona* now considered to be his is the *Angel in Red*, one of the two lateral panels also in the National Gallery. Among Leonardo's pupils in the 1490s, Marco d'Oggiono and Boltraffio have also been proposed as his collaborators (Pietro C. Marani, *Leonardo. Una Carriera di Pittore*, Milan, 1999, pp. 137–55). A more likely candidate, perhaps, is Francesco Napoletano, who painted the other *Angel in Green* (Brown, *Art and Devotion*, 2003, p. 48). Francesco's Madonna in the Zürich Kunsthaus directly translates the *Virgin of the Rocks* into a half-length format. Kenneth Clark already proposed the author of this Madonna as Leonardo's assistant (*Leonardo da Vinci. An Account of his Development as an Artist*, Cambridge, 1939, p. 143).

[21] Larry Keith, "The Virgin of the Rocks," in *Leonardo*, eds. Syson and Keith, 2011, pp. 63–71.

[22] On Leonardo and optics, see *Leonardo da Vinci and Optics. Theory and Practice*, eds. Francesca Fiorani and Alessandro Nova, Venice, 2013; and Francesca Fiorani, *The Shadow Drawing. How Science Taught Leonardo How to Paint*, New York, 2020.

[23] See, with a later dating, Quattrini, *Luini*, 2019, cat. 83, pp. 269–70.

[24] Marilyn Arenberg Lavin, "Giovannino Battista: A Study in Renaissance Religious Symbolism," in *The Art Bulletin*, vol. XXXVII, no. 2, June 1955, pp. 85–101; and vol. XLIII, no, 4, Dec. 1961, pp. 319–26. For the source see Domenico Cavalca, *Vite scelte de' santi padri*, ed. Francesco Costero, Milan, 1879, pp. 233–39.

[25] On the so-called Burlington cartoon, see Syson in *Leonardo*, eds. Syson and Keith, 2011, cat. 86, pp. 288–91; and Vincent Delieuvin in *Saint Anne. Leonardo da Vinci's Ultimate Masterpiece* (ex. Musée du Louvre), ed. Vincent Delieuvin, Paris, 2012, cat. 11, pp. 56–59, both with a date of ca. 1500. Favoring a later dating for the cartoon of ca. 1506–08 is Carmen C. Bambach. "Leonardo's *St. Anne* Types and the Dating of the National Gallery Cartoon," in *Leonardo in Britain. Collections and Historical Reception* (Conference Proceedings, London, 2016), eds. Juliana Barone and Susanna Avery-Quash, Florence, 2019, pp. 59–71.

[26] The British Museum sketches offer the best evidence for the later date for the cartoon. See Carmen C. Bambach, *Leonardo da Vinci Master Draftsman* (exh. Metropolitan Museum of Art), ed. Carmen C. Bambach, New York, 2003, cat. 96, pp. 525–28. Syson (in *Leonardo*, eds. Syson and Keith, 2011, cat. 85, pp. 284–85) and Delieuvin (in *Saint Anne*, ed. Delieuvin, 2012, cat, 10, pp. 53–56) date both works ca. 1500. Either way the cartoon was available to Luini during Leonardo's second Milanese period.

[27] Citing the cartoon, Marani (*Leonardo*, 1999, pp. 262–66) claims that Leonardo studied antique statuary on a presumed trip to Rome at the turn of the century.

[28] *Saint Anne*, ed. Delieuvin, 2012, cat. 66, pp. 205–08.

[29] Villata, *Leonardo*, 1999, doc. 256, pp. 221–23.

[30] About the fresco see: Maria Teresa Binaghi Olivari, in *Disegni e dipinti leonardeschi dalle collezioni milanesi*

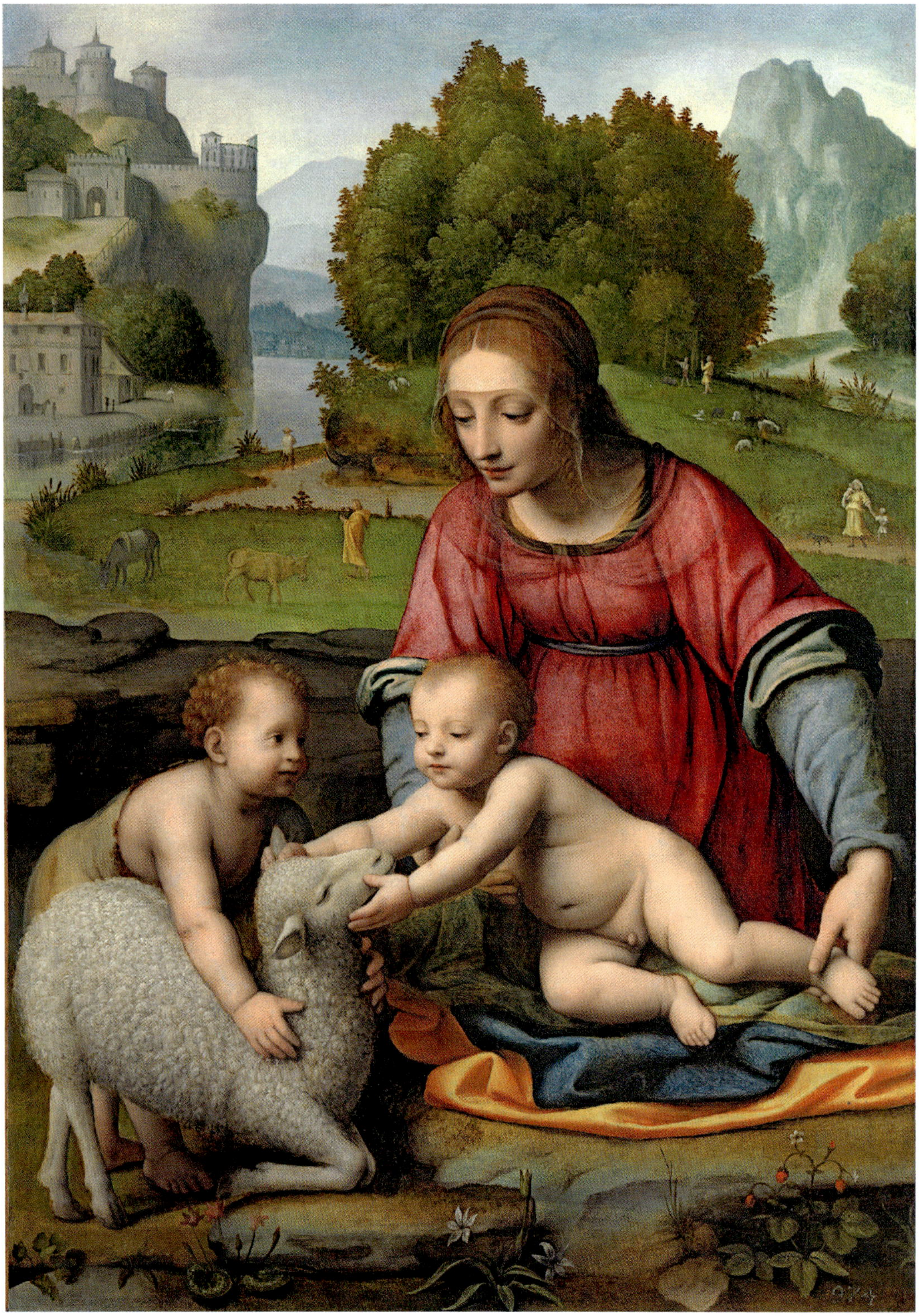

Fig. 42. Bernardino Luini, *Virgin and Child with the Infant Saint John the Baptist and a Lamb*, Museo Thyssen-Bornemisza, Madrid

(exh. Palazzo Reale), Milan, 1987, cat. 71, pp. 142–43; Roberto Cara in *Luini*, eds. Agosti and Stoppa, 2014, vol. 1, cat. 51, pp. 238–41; and Quattrini, *Luini*, cat. 59, pp. 224–26. The author would like to thank Claudio Giorgione and Ida Morisetti for facilitating his study of the picture.

[31] Marco Carminati, *Cesare da Sesto 1477–1523*, Milan & Rome, 1994, cat. 12, pp. 153–56; and Andrea di Lorenzo in *Leonardo in Francia. Il maestro e gli allievi 500 anni dopo la traversata delle Alpi 1516–2016* (exh. Ambasciata d'Italia), ed. Stefania Tullio Cataldo, Paris, 2016, pp. 336–55.

[32] Vasari (*Vite*, ed. Milanesi, vol. IV, 1879, p. 38) describes a cartoon of the Virgin and Child with Saint Anne by Leonardo that included both the infant Baptist and the lamb, but his account (not eyewitness) seems to conflate more than one version of the theme. Scholars have detected the presence of a lamb on the British Museum sheet of sketches for the London cartoon, but there is no agreement on this point.

[33] For the study for the head of Christ in the Accademia, Venice, see Pietro C. Marani in *Leonardo*, ed. Bambach, 2003, cat. 62, pp. 423–26.

[34] Leonardo's composition of Christ Carrying the Cross, cited in the previous note, was known to Solario, who took it as a model for his own treatments of the theme, which in turn influenced Luini. For Solario, see David Alan Brown, *Andrea Solario*, Milan, 1987, cat. 20, p. 143, cat. 57, p. 280, and cat. 72, p. 286; and for Luini, see Quattrini, *Luini*, 2019, cat. 109, pp. 297–99.

[35] Brown, *Solario*, 1987, cat. 31, p. 149. For Luini's variant in the Wallraf-Richartz Museum, Cologne, see Brown, *Solario*, 1987, pp. 255, 277; and Quattrini, *Luini*, 2019, cat. 147, pp. 380–81.

[36] Marco Flamine in *Luini*, eds. Agosti and Stoppa, 2014, cat. 15, pp. 112–21; and Quattrini, *Luini*, 2019, cat. 48, pp. 207–13.

[37] Benedetta Spadaccini in *Luini*, eds. Agosti and Stoppa, vol. I, 2014, cat. 21, pp. 146–47; and Quattrini, *Luini*, cat. 7, pp. 433–34.

[38] About Foppa's destroyed altarpiece, formerly in the Kaiser Friedrich Museum, Berlin, see Mauro Natale in *Pittura a Milano. Rinascimento e Manierismo*, ed. Mina Gregori, Milan, 1998, p. 220 and fig. 45.

[39] The motif of the hysterical woman reappears in Zenale's *Lamentation* in the church of San Giovanni Evangelista, Brescia, cited as a source for Luini's drawing by Quattrini (see the preceding note and Cristina Quattrini, *Brera mai vista. Lo Schermo di Cam. Un dipinto riscoperto di Bernardino Luini*, Milan, 2006, pp. 25–26 and figs. 13–15). The Lombard painter/architect Zenale (ca. 1460–1526) provides another link between Leonardo and Luini: he was friendly with the former, according to Vasari and Lomazzo, and associated with the latter in 1516 (Quattrini, *Luini*, 2019, p. 45). Luini and Zenale appear to have collaborated on the large *Annunciation*, attributed to one or the other, in the Brera, with the Archangel Gabriel and all but one of the airborne angels by Bernardino and the rest of the painting, including the elaborate architectural setting, by Bernardo. The older artist's *Virgin and Child with Saints*, of 1510, formerly in San Francesco Grande and now in the Denver Art Museum, features a kind of architectural grotto inspired by Leonardo's altarpiece in the same church.

[40] Brown, *Solario*, 1987, pp. 99, 105–06, 110, and cat. 28, pp. 147–48.

[41] Brown, *Solario*, 1987, cat. 29, p. 148, and fig. 93.

[42] About the painting, which seems to have influenced Zenale's so-called *Pala Busti*, completed between 1515 and 1518, also in the Brera (Quattrini, *Brera*, 2006, pp. 26–28 and figs. 5, 16–18), see Chiara Battezzati and Giovanni Renzi in *Luini*, eds. Agosti and Stoppa, 2014, vol. 1, cat. 20, pp. 138–42; and Quattrini, *Luini*, 2019, cat. 45, pp. 203–05. Other motifs in the *Lamentation* recur in Luini's fresco of the subject in the nuns' choir of the church of San Maurizio al Monastero Maggiore, Milan (Quattrini, *Luini*, 2019, cat. 71b, pp. 244–45); the predella of the Trivulzio altarpiece in the Duomo of Como (Quattrini, *Luini*, 2019, cat. 50, pp. 214–15); the predella of the San Magno polyptych, Legnano (Quattrini, *Luini*, cat. 113, pp. 302–03); and the Lamentation scene in the background of the *Crucifixion* in Lugano (Quattrini, *Luini*, 2019, cat. 142.08, p. 365).

[43] Patrizio Aiello in *Luini*, eds. Agosti and Stoppa, 2014, vol.1, cat. 22, pp. 148–50; and Quattrini, *Luini*, 2019, cat. 47, pp. 206–07.

[44] Bora in *Legacy*, eds. Bora et al., 1998, p. 344.

[45] Carolyn Wilson, "Focus on Luini's Houston Pieta," in *Arte Lombarda*, vol. CXII, no. 1, 1995, pp. 39–42; and Carolyn Wilson, *Italian Paintings. XV–XVI Centuries in the Museum of Fine Arts, Houston*, London, 1996, cat. 29, pp. 300–3.

[46] Cristina Fraccaro in *Ambrogio da Fossano detto il Bergognone: un Pittore per la Certosa* (exh. Certosa di Pavia), ed. G. C. Sciola, Milan, 1998, cat. 61, pp. 336–37.

[47] Bora in *Legacy*, eds. Bora et al., 1998, pp. 342–44; Giovanni Renzi in *Luini*, eds. Agosti and Stoppa, 2014, vol. 2, cat. 5, pp. 43–46; and Quattrini, *Luini*, 2019, cat. 50, pp. 214–17. Trivulzio, wearing a cardinal's vestment, was raised to the purple in 1517 and stepped down as bishop the following year (Binaghi Olivari, *Luini*, 2007, p. 25).

[48] About this work, see Quattrini, *Luini*, 2019, cat. 121, pp. 328–30. Tatiana Kustodieva (in *Leonardeschi. Da Foppa al Giampietrino. Dipinti dall'Ermitage di San Pietroburgo e dai Musei Civici di Pavia* [exh. Castello Visconteo], eds. Tatiana Kustodieva and Susanna Zatti, Pavia, 2011, cat. I.15, pp. 60–61) notes that the figure of Saint John was inspired by Leonardo's Saint Phillip.

[49] Sotheby's, New York, Jan. 25, 2007, lot 34, pp. 86–89; and Vincent Delieuvin in *Leonardo in Francia*, ed. Cataldo, 2016, pp. 282–91.

[50] Janice Shell, "Gian Giacomo Caprotti, called Salai," in *Legacy*, eds. Bora et al., 1998, pp. 397–406.

[51] Bertrand Jestaz, "François Ier, Salai, et les tableaux de Léonard," in *Revue de l'Art*, vol. 126, no. 4, 1999, pp. 68–72.

[52] Villata, *Documenti*, 1999, no. 323, pp. 275–78, translated into English in *Leonardo on Painting*, ed. Martin Kemp, New Haven & London, 1989, pp. 275–78.

[53] Vasari, *Vite*, ed. Milanesi, vol. IV, 1879, pp. 34–35.

[54] Villata, *Documenti, 1999*, no. *32*, pp. 284–85.

[55] Pietro C. Marani, "A New Date for Francesco Melzi's *Young Man with a Parrot*," in *The Burlington Magazine*, vol. CXXXI, no. 1036, July 1989, pp. 479–81. About Melzi, see Pietro C. Marani in *Legacy*, eds. Bora et al., 1998, pp. 371–84; Francesco Sorce, "Melzi, Francesco," in *Dizionario Biografico degli Italiani*, vol. 73, 2009, pp. 392–94; and Carmen C. Bambach, *Leonardo da Vinci Rediscovered*, 4 vols., New Haven & London, 2019, vol. III, pp. 519–33 and 591–94.

[56] Thanks to Curators Neville Rowley and Roberto Contini for the information that the signature, reported by Mariette in the eighteenth century, on the stone near Vertumnus's left foot, is now effaced except for two letters.

[57] *Leonardo*, ed. Bambach, 2003, cat. 120, pp. 640–41.

[58] Bambach, *Leonardo*, 2019, vol. III, pp. 287–88 and 524–26. Leonardo's notes on the verso, dated by Bambach to ca. 1510, apparently preceded Melzi's study of a foot and Leonardo's adjacent on-the-spot sketch of a mountain on the recto. The sheet seems to have been reused first by Melzi and then by Leonardo. The author dates the painting ca. 1520.

[59] Tatiana Kustodieva (*Flora Restored. Francesco Melzi's Flora, its history and recent restoration* [Hermitage Foundation UK], London, 2021) reports that the original signature in Greek letters can no longer be detected on the painting. The partial or full removal of Melzi's name on the Berlin and Hermitage pictures suggests that their owners wished to upgrade them to be by Leonardo (Emily Burns, *Leonardo's Legacy: Francesco Melzi and the Leonardeschi*, www.nationalgallery.org.uk).

[60] About Leonardo's botanical studies, also meant to illustrate his proposed *Treatise on Painting*, see William A. Emboden, *Leonardo da Vinci on Plants and Gardens*, Portland, Oregon, 1987; and Francis Ames-Lewis, "Leonardo's Botanical Drawings," in *Achademia Leonardi Vinci. Journal of Leonardo Studies & Bibliography of Vinciana*, vol. X, 1997, pp. 117–24.

[61] On Melzi as a copyist of Leonardo's botanical studies, see Bambach, *Leonardo*, 2019, vol. III, p. 530 and pl. 13.47.

[62] Bambach, *Leonardo*, 2019, vol. III, p. 592, and vol. IV, notes 40, 41 on pp. 420–21.

[63] One of the copies was auctioned at Christie's, London, 4 July 2012, lot 108. Having been acquired for a very large sum, this version of the composition was juxtaposed with the original in the Hermitage in 2016. Another fine copy, formerly in the Holford Collection, Dorchester House, London, where it was attributed to Luini, is in the Virginia Museum of Fine Arts, Richmond, Virginia. My thanks to Curator Sylvain Cordier for the opportunity to examine this work.

[64] Marina Minozzi in *Leonardo in Francia. Il Maestro e gli Allievi 500*

Anni dopo la Traversata delle Alpi, 1516–2016 (exh. Italian Embassy), ed. Stefania Tullio Cataldo, Paris, 2016, pp. 292–305; and Vincent Delieuvin in *La Goconde Nue* (exh. Musée Condé, Chantilly), ed. Vincent Delieuvin, Paris, 2019, cat. 13, pp. 98–107. Another source for this work would seem to be the so-called *Monna Vanna* in a Swiss private collection, attributed to Salai (Carlo Pedretti in *Il Cinquecento Lombardo. Da Leonardo a Caravaggio* [exh. Palazzo Reale], ed. Flavio Caroli, Milan, 2000, cat. III.33, pp. 136–37.

[65] Quattrini, *Luini*, 2019, cat. 28, pp. 448–49.

[66] Bambach, *Leonardo*, 2003, cat. 75, pp. 463–65.

[67] On the grotesque heads in general, see Martin Clayton, *Leonardo da Vinci. The Divine and the Grotesque* (exh. The Queen's Gallery, Holyrood House, Edinburgh, and Buckingham Palace), London, 2002; and Bambach, *Leonardo*, 2019, vol. I, pp. 457–72.

[68] Clayton, *Grotesque*, 2002, cat. 38, pp. 88–89; and *Leonardo*, ed. Bambach, 2003, pp. 526–27.

[69] Bambach, *Leonardo*, 2019, vol. III, pp. 595–96 and pl. 14.9, showing the sheet before restoration, and vol. IV, p. 423 note 68. The detached fragment with the man's profile was unaccountably rejected by Quattrini (*Luini*, 2019, cat. 38, pp. 456–57).

[70] Lomazzo, *Scritti*, ed. Ciardi, vol. I, 1973, p. 290, and vol. II, 1974, p. 315.

[71] Bambach, *Leonardo*, 2019, vol. III, p. 568 and pl. 13.85.

[72] Two "nutcracker" profiles appear on a sheet of studies by Luini (Quattrini, *Luini*. 2019, cat. 35, pp. 454–55).

[73] Quattrini, *Luini*, 2019, cat. 163, pp. 400–2.

[74] Giulio Bora in *Pinacoteca Ambrosiana. 1. Dipinti dal medioevo alla Metà del Cinquecento*, ed. Luciano Caramel, Milan, 2005, cat. 49, pp. 162–65; Giovanni Agosti and Jacopo Stoppa in *Luini*, eds. Agosti and Stoppa, 2014, vol. I, cat. 79, pp. 312–15; and Quattrini, *Luini*, 2019, cat. 161, pp. 396–98.

[75] Lomazzo, *Scritti*, ed. Ciardi, vol. II, 1974, p. 150.

[76] On the hypothetical provenance from Leonardo to Melzi and from him to Bernardino and Aurelio Luini, see Bambach, *Leonardo*, 2019, vol. IV, note 173, p. 314.

[77] Pamela M. Jones, *Federico Borromeo and the Ambrosiana. Art Patronage and Reform in Seventeenth-Century Milan*, Cambridge, MA, 1993.

[78] Pamela M. Jones, "Defining the Canonical Status of Milanese Renaissance Art: Bernardino Luini's Paintings for the Ambrosian Accademia del Disegno," in *Arte Lombarda*, vol. C, no. 1, 1992, pp. 89–94. The group includes Luini's *Magdalen* in the National Gallery of Art, Washington, DC. The picture is based on a composition by Leonardo known from two framed sketches in the Courtauld Institute Gallery, London. See Pamela M. Jones, "Bernardino Luini's Magdalene from the Collection of Federico Borromeo. Religious Contemplation and Iconographic Sources," in *Studies in the History of Art*, National Gallery of Art, Washington, DC, vol. 24, 1990, pp. 67–72. Luke Syson (in *Leonardo*, eds. Syson and Keith, 2011, cat. 9, pp. 108–09) adds that both sketches show the subject lifting the lid of her ointment jar, as in the painting. Luini's source is likely to have been a more finished version, possibly a cartoon. In that sense the *Magdalen* might be considered a stand-in for a picture that Leonardo never painted.

[79] Federico Borromeo, *Sacred Painting. Museum*, ed. and trans. Kenneth S. Rothwell Jr. with an introduction and notes by Pamela M. Jones, The I Tatti Renaissance Library Series, Cambridge, MA & London, 2010, pp. 174–77, also quoted in Alessandro Morandotti, "Il revival leonardesco nell'età di Federico Borromeo," in *I leonardeschi a Milano. Fortuna e collezionismo*, eds. Maria Teresa Fiorio and Pietro C. Marani, Milan, 1991, pp. 169–70 (166–82).

[80] Jones in *Arte Lombarda*, 1992, pp. 91–93.

[81] Except for Agosti and Stoppa in *Luini*, 2014, vol. I, p. 315.

[82] Syson in *Leonardo*, eds. Syson and Keith, 2011, pp. 289–90; and Bambach, *Leonardo*, 2019, vol. III, pp. 36–38.

[83] Agosti and Stoppa in *Luini*, eds. Agosti and Stoppa, 2014, vol. I, cat. 79, pp. 312–17.

[84] Quattrini, *Luini*, 2019, cat. 161, pp. 396–98. Bambach (*Leonardo*, 2019, vol. III, pp. 36–38, and vol. IV, p. 314 note 175) reaffirms the traditional attribution to Luini and dates the painting to ca. 1520. Aurelio's style differs completely from his father's while those of his three older brothers are unknown.

[85] Bora in *Legacy*, eds. Bora et al., 1998, p. 354.

[86] Agosti in *Luini*, eds. Agosti and Stoppa, 2014, vol. I, cat. 56, pp. 258–60; and Quattrini, *Luini*, 2019, cat. 138, pp. 351–52.

[87] Quattrini, *Luini*, 2019, cat. 144, pp. 375–76, Luini's depiction of the theme in the National Gallery of Canada, Ottowa, also includes both infants (Quattrini, 2019, cat. 136. pp. 349–50).

[88] *Leonardo*, ed. Bambach, 2003, cat. 94, pp. 515–20; and Bambach, *Leonardo*, 2019, vol. III, pp. 15–24.

[89] Quattrini, *Luini*, 2019, cat. 162, pp. 398–400, as by a Luini follower ca. 1530. My thanks to Prado director Miguel Falomir and conservator Almudena Sánchez Martín for facilitating my study of the picture while it was undergoing treatment in 2020. Except for the partly overcleaned dark background and some small scattered losses, the condition is very good, especially the flesh tones allowing for an appreciation of the artist's chiaroscuro. The cross staff below the Baptist was removed as a later addition (conservator's report of 23 March 2022).

[90] Alessandro Bettagno, "Italian Painting," in Alessandro Bettagno, Christopher Brown, Francisco Calvo Serraller, Francis Haskell, and Alfonso E. Pérez Sanchez, *The Prado Museum*, Madrid, 1996, pp. 226–29.

[91] Pietro C. Marani, *Leonardo e i Leonardeschi a Brera*, Florence, 1987, cat. 40, pp. 214–17.

[92] Giovanni Agosti, *Disegni del Rinascimento in Valpadana* (exh. Gabinetto di Disegni e Stampe, Galleria degli Uffizi), Florence, 2001, cat. 43, pp. 223–26; and Quattrini, *Luini*, 2019, cat. 2, pp. 429–30. Both authors date the drawing to the early 1510s.

[93] Bambach, *Leonardo*, 2019, vol. I, pp. 284–85. Unlike the other sketches on the sheet, this one has more nuanced left-handed shading and a rocky landscape setting for the figures.

[94] The composition was popular with Leonardo's pupil Marco d'Oggiono and with Joos Van Cleve, known as the "Leonardo of the North." See Franco Moro, "Spunti sulla diffusione di un tema leonardesco tra Italia e Fiandra sino a Lanino," in *Leonardeschi*, eds. Fiorio and Marani, 1991, pp. 120–40; Laura Traversi, "Il tema dei due fanciulli che si baciano e abbacciano tra leonardismo italiano e leonardismo fiammingo," in *Raccolta Vinciana*, vol. XXVII, 1997, pp. 373–437; and Dan Ewing, "Joos Van Cleve und Leonardo: Italienische Kunst in Niederländische Übersetzung," in *Joos Van Cleve. Leonardo des Nordens* (exh. Suermundt-Ludwig-Museum, Aachen), ed. Peter Van den Brink, Stuttgart, 2011, pp. 112–31.

[95] Quattrini (*Luini*, 2019, cat. 41, p. 459) attributes the drawing but not the painting for which it was made to Luini.

[96] Chiara Battezzati in *Luini*, eds. Agosti and Stoppa, 2014, vol. 1, cat. 27, pp. 168–71; and Quattrini, *Luini*, 2019, cat. 89, pp. 275–76.

[97] Brown, *Art and Devotion*, 2003, pp. 76–77; and Quattrini, *Luini*, 2019, cat. 53, pp. 219–20. Compare also Luini's contemporary fresco of the same subject in the Certosa di Pavia (Simone Bertelli in Luini, eds. Agosti and Stoppa, vol. II, cat. 3, pp. 34–36; and Quattrini, *Luini*, 2019, cat. 23, pp. 172–73). The motif of the Christ Child reaching for a flower was introduced into Milan by Leonardo, and adopted by Solario and other members of his circle in the 1490s.

[98] Giovanni Agosti in *Luini*, eds. Agosti and Stoppa, 2014, vol. I, cat. 40, pp. 210–13; and Quattrini, *Luini*, 2019, cat. 156, pp. 389–90.

[99] Michael Swicklik, Barbara H. Berrie, and Gretchen Hirschauer, "*Sfumato* and Sheen. Bernardino Luini's *Lady in Black*," in *Facture*, National Gallery of Art, Washington, DC, vol. 2, eds. Daphne Barbour and E. Melanie Gifford, 2015, pp. 140–57.

[100] Bora in *Legacy*, eds. Bora et al., 1998, pp. 368–69.

[101] For a contemporary copy made while the original was underway and now in the Museo del Prado, see *Leonardo y la copia de Mona Lisa del Museo del Prado, Nuevos planteamientos sobre las practicas del taller vinciano* (exh. Museo del Prado), ed. Ana González Mozo, Madrid, 2021. The cartoon for *Mona Lisa* is lost, though one exists for the variant known as *La Joconde Nue* in the Musée Condé at Chantilly.

[102] *Leonardo*, ed. Bambach, 2003, cat. 131, pp. 663–66; Claudio Gulli in *Luini*, eds. Agosti and Stoppa, 2014, vol. I, cat. 44, pp. 219–20; Quattrini, *Luini*, 2019, cat. 29, pp. 449–50; and Bambach, *Leonardo*, 2019, vol. II, pp. 256–62.

[103] Bambach, *Leonardo*, 2019, vol. II, pp. 253–62.

[104] Hirschauer (in *Facture*, eds. Barbour and Gifford, 2015) describes the costume in detail.

[105] Parmigianino's so-called *Schiava Turca* in the Galleria Nazionale, Parma,

for example, or Lotto's *Lucina Brembate* in the Accademia Carrara, Bergamo, to which Luini's portrait has often been compared.

[106] Brown, *Solario*, 1987, pp. 236–38 and cat. 69, p. 285.

[107] Stefano Bruzzese in *Luini*, eds. Agosti and Stoppa, 2014, vol. II, cat. 7, pp. 55–59; and Quattrini, *Luini*, 2019, cat. 113, pp. 301–05. Thanks to Giuseppe Rovera for facilitating my inspection of the altarpiece.

[108] A renewed interest in Leonardo's altarpiece on Luini's part in the 1520s is possibly reflected by the copy of the *Virgin of the Rocks* in the parish church of Santa Giustina in Affori. Once claimed as Leonardo's, this smaller version of the original has a color scheme, facial types, symbolic plants, and even a sleeping Joseph in the background – typical of Luini. Of mediocre quality, the picture appears to be a copy of a lost work by him or a product of his shop. See *Leonardo da Vinci. The European Genius. Paintings and Drawings* (exh. Basilica of Kockelberg, Brussels), ed. Carlo Pedretti, Foligno, 2007, cat. 18, pp. 76–77; Luigi Ripamonti, *La Tavola della Vergine delle Rocce in Affori*, Affori (Milan), 2015; and Quattrini, *Luini*, 2019, cat. C8, pp. 425–26.

[109] Quattrini, *Luini*, 2019, cat. 154, pp. 387–88, and cat. 125, pp. 332–33. Luini's *Salome with the Head of the Baptist* in the Uffizi (Claudio Gulli in *Luini*, eds. Agosti and Stoppa, 2014, vol. I, cat. 57, pp. 262–66; and Quattrini, Luini, cat. 133, pp. 346–47) combines the influence of Solario for the composition with that of Leonardo's so called *Scapiliata* in the Galleria Nazionale, Parma (*La fortuna della Scapiliata di Leonardo da Vinci* [exh. Complesso Monumentale della Pilotta], eds. Pietro C. Marani and Simone Verde, Parma, 2019) for the head of the temptress.

[110] Quattrini, *Luini*, 2019, cat. 143, pp. 373–74, and cat. 29, pp. 185–87. Matthew Landrus ("Salvator Mundi: Why Bernardino Luini Should Be Back in the Frame," in *The Art Newspaper*, no. 304, Sept. 2018, p. 6) has recently revived the Luini attribution for Leonardo's *Salvator Mundi*, which it bore in the Cook Collection.

[111] Quattrini, *Luini*, 2019, cat. 165, pp. 403–04.

[112] Mar Borobia, *Museo Thyssen-Bornemisza. Old Masters*, Madrid, 2009, p. 172; and Quattrini, *Luini*, 2019, cat. 102, pp. 291–92.

Bibliography

The authors of articles or essays in books or exhibition catalogues are cited individually by name, while the compilers of catalogue entries in exhibition catalogues are not so cited.

A

Agosti, Giovanni. *Disegni del Rinascimento in Valpadana* (exh. cat., Gabinetto di Disegni e Stampe, Galleria degli Uffizi). Florence, 2001.

Agosti, Giovanni, and Jacopo Stoppa, eds. *Bernardino Luini e i suoi figli* (exh. cat., Palazzo Reale, Milan). 2 vols. Milan, 2014.

Ames-Lewis, Francis. "Leonardo's Botanical Drawings." *Achademia Leonardi Vinci. Journal of Leonardo Studies & Bibliography of Vinciana* X (1997): 117–24.

B

Ballarin, Alessandro. *Leonardo a Milano. Problemi di Leonardismo Milanese tra Quattrocento e Cinquecento.* 4 vols. Verona, 2010.

Bambach, Carmen C., ed. *Leonardo da Vinci Master Draftsman* (exh. cat., Metropolitan Museum of Art). New York, 2003.

Bambach, Carmen C. *Leonardo da Vinci Rediscovered.* 4 vols. New Haven-London, 2019.

Bambach, Carmen C. "Leonardo's St. Anne Types and the Dating of the National Gallery Cartoon." *Leonardo in Britain. Collections and Historical Reception* (Conference Proceedings, London, 2016), eds. Juliana Barone and Susanna Avery-Quash. Florence (2019): 59–71.

Bayer, Andrea. "Defining Naturalism in Lombard Painting." *Painters of Reality. The Legacy of Leonardo and Caravaggio in Lombardy* (exh. cat., Metropolitan Museum of Art), ed. Andrea Bayer. New York, 2004: 2–19.

Beltrami, Luca. *Luini 1512–1532. Materiale di Studio.* Milan, 1911.

Berenson, Bernard. *North Italian Painters of the Renaissance.* New York-London, 1907.

Bettagno, Alessandro. "Italian Painting." *The Prado Museum*, eds. Alessandro Bettagno, Christopher Brown, Francisco Calvo Serraller, Francis Haskell, and Alfonso E. Perez Sanchez. Madrid, 1996: 226–29.

Binaghi Olivari, Maria Teresa. *Bernardino Luini.* Milan, 2007.

Bora, Giulio. "Bernardino Luini." *The Legacy of Leonardo. Painters in Lombardy 1490–1530*, eds. Giulio Bora, Maria Teresa Fiorio, Pietro C. Marani, and Janice Shell. Milan, 1998: 325–70.

Borobia, Mar. *Museo Thyssen-Bornemisza. Old Masters.* Madrid, 2009.

Borromeo, Federico. *Sacred Painting. Museum*, ed. and trans. Kenneth S. Rothwell Jr., with an introduction and notes by Pamela M. Jones, The I Tatti Renaissance Library Series, Cambridge, MA.-London, 2010.

Brown, David Alan. *Andrea Solario.* Milan, 1987.

Brown, David Alan. *Leonardo da Vinci. Art and Devotion in the Madonnas of his Pupils.* Cinisello Balsamo (Milan), 2003.

Burns, Emily. *Leonardo's Legacy: Francesco Melzi and the Leonardeschi.* www.nationalgallery.org.uk.

C

Caramel, Luciano, ed. *Pinacoteca Ambrosiana. 1. Dipinti dal medioevo alla Metà del Cinquecento.* Milan, 2005.

Carminati, Marco. *Cesare da Sesto 1477–1523.* Milan-Rome, 1994.

Caroli, Flavio, ed. *Il Cinquecento Lombardo. Da Leonardo a Caravaggio* (exh. cat., Palazzo Reale, Milan). Milan, 2000.

Cataldo, Stefania Tullio, ed. *Leonardo in Francia. Il maestro e gli allievi 500 anni dopo la traversata delle Alpi 1516–2016* (exh. cat., Ambasciata d'Italia). Paris, 2016.

Cavalca, Domenico. *Vite scelte de' santi padri*, ed. Francesco Costero. Milan, 1879.

Christian, John, "Burne-Jones's Second Italian Journey." *Apollo* CII, no. 165 (November 1975): 334–37.

Clark, Kenneth. *Leonardo da Vinci. An Account of his Development as an Artist.* Cambridge, 1939.

Clayton, Martin. *Leonardo da Vinci. The Divine and the Grotesque* (exh. cat., The Queen's Gallery Holyrood House, Edinburgh, and Buckingham Palace, London). London, 2002.

Clayton, Martin. *Leonardo da Vinci. A Life in Drawing.* London-New York, 2018.

Cook, Herbert, ed. *Illustrated Catalogue of Pictures by Masters of the Milanese and Allied Schools of Lombardy* (exh. cat., Burlington Fine Arts Club, 1898). London, 1899.

D

Delieuvin, Vincent, ed. *Saint Anne. Leonardo da Vinci's Ultimate Masterpiece* (exh. cat., Musée du Louvre, Paris). Paris, 2012.

Delieuvin, Vincent, ed., *La Gioconde Nue* (exh. cat., Musée Condé, Chantilly). Paris, 2019.

Disegni e dipinti leonardeschi dalle collezioni milanesi (exh. cat., Palazzo Reale, Milan). Milan 1987.

E

Emboden, William A. *Leonardo da Vinci on Plants and Gardens.* Portland, Oregon, 1987.

Ewing, Dan. "Joos Van Cleve und Leonardo: Italienische Kunst in Niederlandische Ubersetzung." *Joos van Cleve. Leonardo des Nordens* (exh. cat., Suermundt-Ludwig-Museum, Aachen), ed. Peter Van den Brink. Stuttgart, 2011: 112–31.

F

Finaldi, Gabriele, ed. *The Image of Christ.* London, 2000.

Fiorani, Francesca, and Alessandro Nova, eds. *Leonardo da Vinci and Optics. Theory and Practice.* Venice, 2013.

Fiorani, Francesca. *The Shadow Drawing. How Science Taught Leonardo How to Paint.* New York, 2020.

Freedberg, Sydney J. *Painting in Italy 1500 to 1600.* Pelican History of Art Series, Harmondsworth, 1971.

G

González Mozo, Anna, ed. *Leonardo y la copia de Mona Lisa del Museo del Prado. Nuevos planteamientos sobre las prácticas del taller vinciano* (exh. cat., Museo del Prado, Madrid). Madrid, 2021.

Gregori, Mina, ed. *Pittura a Milano. Rinascimento e Manierismo.* Milan, 1998.

H

Hall, Nicholas, and Virginia Brilliant. *Faithful to Nature. Eleven Lombard Paintings 1530–1760*. New York, 2019.

Harrison, Colin, and Christopher Newall. *The Pre-Raphaelites and Italy* (exh. cat., Ashmolean Museum, Oxford). Oxford, 2010.

J

Jestaz, Bertrand. "François Ier, Salai, et les tableaux de Léonard." *Revue de l'Art* 126, no. 4 (1999): 68–72.

Jones, Pamela M. "Bernardino Luini's Magdalene from the Collection of Federico Borromeo, Religious Contemplation and Iconographic Source." *Studies in the History of Art*, National Gallery of Art, Washington, DC 24 (1990): 67–72.

Jones, Pamela, M. "Defining the Canonical Status of Milanese Art: Bernardino Luini's Paintings for the Ambrosian Accademia del Disegno." *Arte Lombarda* C, no 1 (1992): 89–94.

Jones, Pamela M. *Federico Borromeo and the Ambrosiana. Art Patronage and Reform in Seventeenth-Century Milan*. Cambridge, MA, 1993.

K

Katz, Melissa R, ed. *Divine Mirrors. The Virgin Mary in the Visual Arts* (exh. cat., Davis Museum and Cultural Center, Wellesley College). New York, 2001.

Kemp, Martin, ed. *Leonardo on Painting*, New Haven-London, 1989.

Kugler, Franz Theodor. *Handbook of Painting. The Italian Schools*, ed. Charles Lock Eastlake. 2 vols. London, 1869.

Kustodieva, Tatiana, and Susanna Zatti, eds. *Leonardeschi. Da Foppa al Giampietrino. Dipinti dall'Ermitage di San Pietroburgo a dai Musei Civici di Pavia* (exh. cat., Castello Visconteo, Pavia). Pavia, 2011.

Kustodieva, Tatiana. *Flora Restored. Francesco Melzi's Flora, its history and recent restoration*. London, 2021.

L

Landrus, Matthew. "Salvator Mundi: Why Bernardino Luini Should Be Back in the Frame." *The Art Newspaper*, no. 304 (Sept. 2018): 6.

Lanzi, Luigi. *Storia Pittorica della Italia dal Risorgimento delle Belle Arti fin presso la Fine del XVIII Secolo*, ed. Martino Capucci. 3 vols. Florence, 1968–74.

Lavin, Marilyn Arenberg. "Giovannino Battista: A Study in Renaissance Religious Symbolism." *The Art Bulletin* XXXVII, no. 2 (June 1955): 85–101; and XLIII, no. 4 (December 1961): 319–26.

Lomazzo, Giovanni Paolo. *Scritti sull'arte*, ed. Roberto Paolo Ciardi. 2 vols. 1973–75.

Longhi, Roberto. *Officina Ferrarese, 1934. Seguito dagli Ampliamenti 1940 e dai Nuovi Ampliamenti 1940–55*. Florence, 1956.

M

Marani, Pietro C. *Leonardo e i leonardeschi a Brera*. Florence, 1987.

Marani, Pietro C. "A New Date for Francesco Melzi's *Young Man with a Parrot*." *The Burlington Magazine* CXXXI. No. 1036 (July 1989): 479–81.

Marani, Pietro C. "Francesco Melzi." *The Legacy of Leonardo. Painters in Lombardy 1490–1530*, eds. Giulio Bora, Maria Teresa Fiorio, Pietro C. Marani, and Janice Shell. Milan 1998: 371–84.

Marani, Pietro C. "Luini, Bernardino." *Dizionario Biografico degli Italiani* LXVI (2006): 510–18.

Marani, Piero C. *Bernardino Luini. Una Carriera di Pittore e un Dipinto Inedito*. Olgiate Olona, 2007.

Marani, Pietro C. *Leonardo da Vinci. The Complete Paintings*. New York, 2019.

Marani, Pietro C., and Simone Verde. *La fortuna della Scapiliata di Leonado da Vinci* (exh. cat., Complesso Monumentale della Pilotta, Parma). Parma, 2019.

Morandotti, Alessandro. "Il revival leonardesco nell'età di Federico Borromeo." *I Leonardeschi a Milano. Fortuna e collezionismo*, eds. Maria Teresa Fiorio and Pietro C. Marani (Acts of the Conference, 1990). Milan, 1991: 166–82.

Moro, Franco, "Spunti sulla diffusione di un tema leonardesco tra Italia e Fiandra fino a Lanino." *I Leonardeschi a Milano. Fortuna e Collezionismo*," eds. Maria Teresa Fiorio and Pietro C. Marani (Acts of the Conference, 1990). Milan, 1991: 120–40.

N

Newall, Christopher, ed. *The Pre-Raphaelites and Italy* (exh. cat., Ashmolean Museum). Oxford, 2010.

Ottino Della Chiesa, Angela. *Bernardino Luini*. Novara, 1956.

P

Pedretti, Carlo, ed. *Leonardo da Vinci. The European Genius. Paintings and Drawings* (exh. cat. Basilica of Kockelberg, Brussels). Foligno, 2007.

Q

Quattrini, Cristina. "Lo Schermo di Cam." *Brera mai vista. Lo Schermo di Cam. Un dipinto riscoperto di Bernardino Luini* (exh. cat., Pinacoteca di Brera), ed. Cristina Quattrini. Milan, 2006: 8–47.

Quattrini, Cristina. "Una Deposizione dalla croce di Bernardo Zenale." *Nuovi Studi* 13 (2007): 51–55.

Quattrini, Cristina. *Bernardino Luini*. Milan, 2019.

R

Rinaldi, Furio. "The 'Academia Leonardi Vinci'. Leonardo's Pupils, Followers and the Legacy of the Master's Works." *Leonardo da Vinci 1452–1519. The Design of the World* (exh. cat., Palazzo Reale) eds. Pietro C. Marani and Maria Teresa Fiorio. Milan, 2015: 438–49.

Rio, Alexis-François. *Leonardo da Vinci e la sua Scuola*, trans. V.G. De Castro. Milan, 1856.

Ripamonti, Luigi. *La Tavola della Vergine delle Rocce in Affori*. Affori (Milan), 2015.

Romano, Giovanni. *Rinascimento in Lombardia. Foppa, Zenale, Leonardo, Bramantino*. Milan, 2011.

Ruskin, John. *The Works of John Ruskin*, eds. E. T. Cook and A. Wedderburn. 39 vols. London, 1903–12.

S

Sciola, G.C., ed. *Ambrogio da Fossano detto il Bergognone: un Pittore per la Certosa* (exh. cat., Certosa di Pavia). Milan, 1998.

Seidel, Linda, ed. *Pious Journeys. Christian Devotional Art and Practice in the Later Middle Ages and Renaissance*. Chicago, 2001.

Shell, Janice. "Gian Giacomo Caprotti, called Salai." *The Legacy of Leonardo. Painters in Lombardy 1490–1530*, eds. Giulio Bora, Maria Teresa Fiorio, Pietro C. Marani, and Janice Shell. Milan, 1998: 397–406.

Sorce, Francesco. "Melzi, Francesco." *Dizionario Biografico degli Italiani* 73 (2009): 392–94.

Swicklik, Michael, Barbara Berrie, and Gretchen Hirschauer. "*Sfumato* and Sheen. Bernardino Luini's *Lady in Black*," *Facture*. National Gallery of Art, Washington, DC 2, eds., Daphne Barbour and E. Melanie Gifford. (2015): 140–57.

Syson, Luke, and Larry Keith, eds. *Leonardo da Vinci. Painter at the Court of Milan* (exh. cat., National Gallery, London). London, 2011.

T

Traversi, Laura. "Il tema dei due fanciulli che si baciano e abbracciano tra leonardismo italiano e leonardismo fiammingo." *Raccolta Vinciana* XXVII (1987): 373–437.

V

Van Os, Henk. *The Art of Devotion in the Late Middle Ages in Europe 1300–1500*. Princeton, 1994.

Vasari, Giorgio. *Le Vite de più Eccellenti Pittori Scultori ed Architettori*, ed. Gaetano Milanesi. 9 vols. Florence, 1878–85.

Venturi, Adolfo. *Storia dell'Arte Italiana. IX. La Pittura del Cinquecento. Parte II*. Milan, 1926.

Villata, Edoardo. *Leonardo da Vinci. I Documenti e le Testimonianze Contemporanee*. Milan, 2019.

W

Williamson, George C. *Bernardino Luini*. London 1899.

Wilson, Carolyn. "Focus on Luini's Houston Pietà." *Arte Lombarda* CXII, no.1 (1995): 39–42.

Wilson, Carolyn. *Italian Paintings. XV–XVI Centuries in the Museum of Fine Arts, Houston*. London, 1996.

Index